S0-AQI-862

A Plastic Bottle's Journey

by Suzanne Slade

illustrated by Nadine Wickenden

PICTURE WINDOW BOOKS

a capstone imprint

Thanks to our advisers for their expertise, research, and advice:

Plastics Division, American Chemistry Council

Moore Recycling Associates, Inc., Sonoma, California

Terry Flaherty, PhD, Professor of English
Minnesota State University, Mankato

Editor: Jill Kalz
Designer: Tracy Davies
Art Director: Nathan Gassman
Production Specialist: Sarah Bennett
The illustrations in this book were created with watercolor and collage fabric.

Picture Window Books
151 Good Counsel Drive
P.O. Box 669
Mankato, MN 56002-0669
877-845-8392
www.capstonepub.com

All books published by Picture Window Books are manufactured with paper containing at least 10 percent post-consumer waste.

Library of Congress Cataloging-in-Publication Data
Slade, Suzanne.
  A plastic bottle's journey / by Suzanne Slade ; illustrated by
Nadine Wickenden.
      p. cm. — (Follow it!)
  Includes index.
  ISBN 978-1-4048-6267-8 (library binding)
  ISBN 978-1-4048-6711-6 (paperback)
  1. Plastic bottles—Recycling. I. Wickenden, Nadine, ill. II. Title.
  TD798.S58 2011
  668.4'97—dc22
                            2010033764

Printed in the United States of America in North Mankato, Minnesota.
092010
005933CGS11

Sssssssss!

Thousands of tiny pellets tumble into a pile. They look like salt or ice crystals. But they're not.

These pellets are bits of plastic. And they're about to be heated up, blown up, and filled up! They're about to be made into something people use every day.

Here's where a plastic bottle's journey begins.

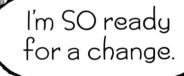

I'm SO ready for a change.

3

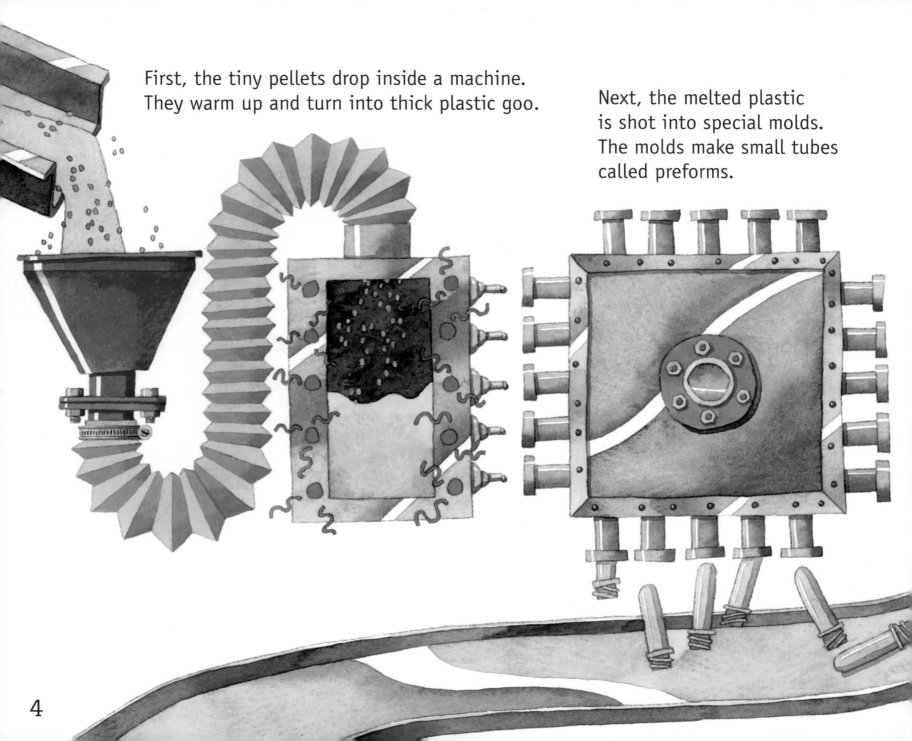

First, the tiny pellets drop inside a machine.
They warm up and turn into thick plastic goo.

Next, the melted plastic
is shot into special molds.
The molds make small tubes
called preforms.

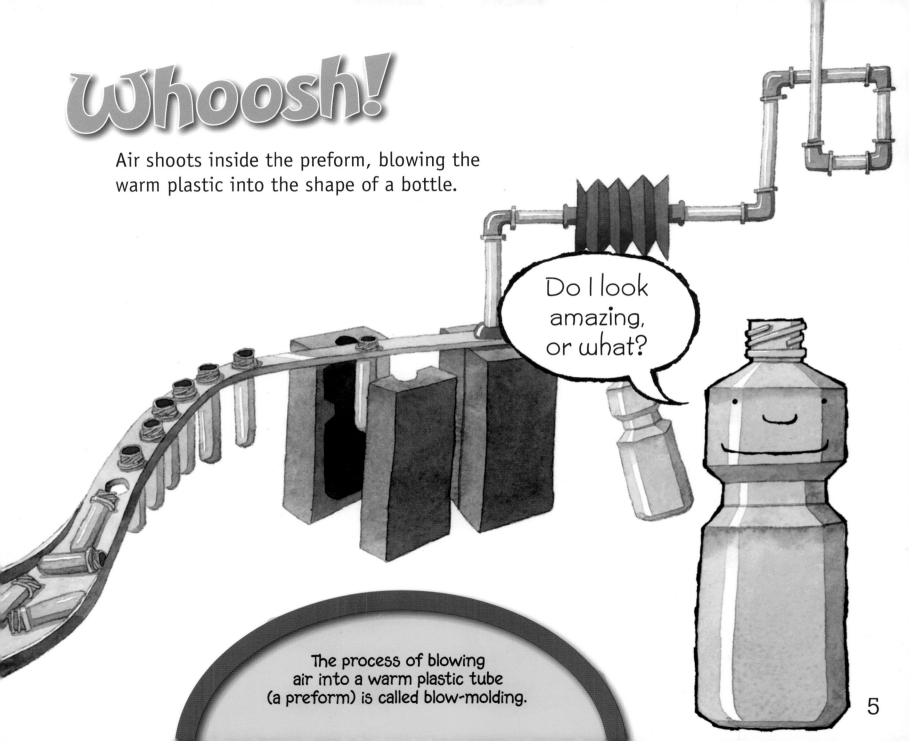

Whoosh!

Air shoots inside the preform, blowing the warm plastic into the shape of a bottle.

Do I look amazing, or what?

The process of blowing air into a warm plastic tube (a preform) is called blow-molding.

5

Vrooom!

Workers load the plastic bottle into a truck with thousands of other new bottles. The empty bottles ride down the highway to another factory.

6

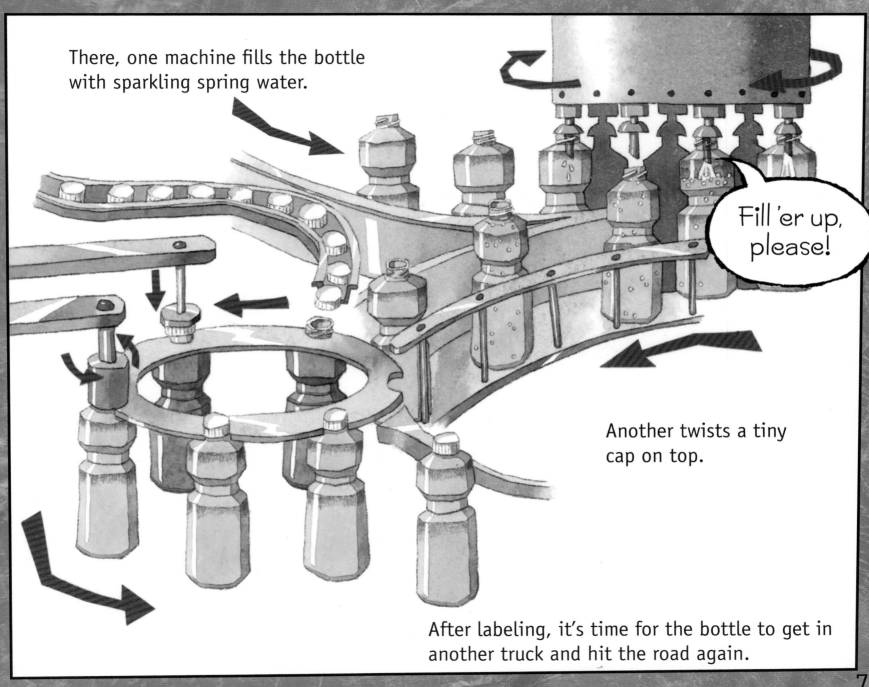

There, one machine fills the bottle with sparkling spring water.

Fill 'er up, please!

Another twists a tiny cap on top.

After labeling, it's time for the bottle to get in another truck and hit the road again.

7

Miles later, the truck driver rolls the plastic bottle into a store. She places it in a refrigerator.

The bottle doesn't sit long. After checking out the different drinks, a boy grabs the bottle. He pays the clerk and dashes out the door. He doesn't want to be late for his big day.

Ooh! Pick me! Pick me!

Americans buy more than 81 million bottles a day. That's nearly 30 billion plastic water bottles a year!

The plastic bottle can't believe its luck—it's field trip day!

After a morning of giant giraffes, slithering snakes, and enormous elephants, everyone is hungry.

The boy grabs the bottle and takes a long drink. **Ahhh!**

And before you can say "H-2-O," the bottle is empty. The boy tosses it into a recycling bin.

Hope to see you again soon!

That night, a big truck carries the bottle to a recycling facility.

12

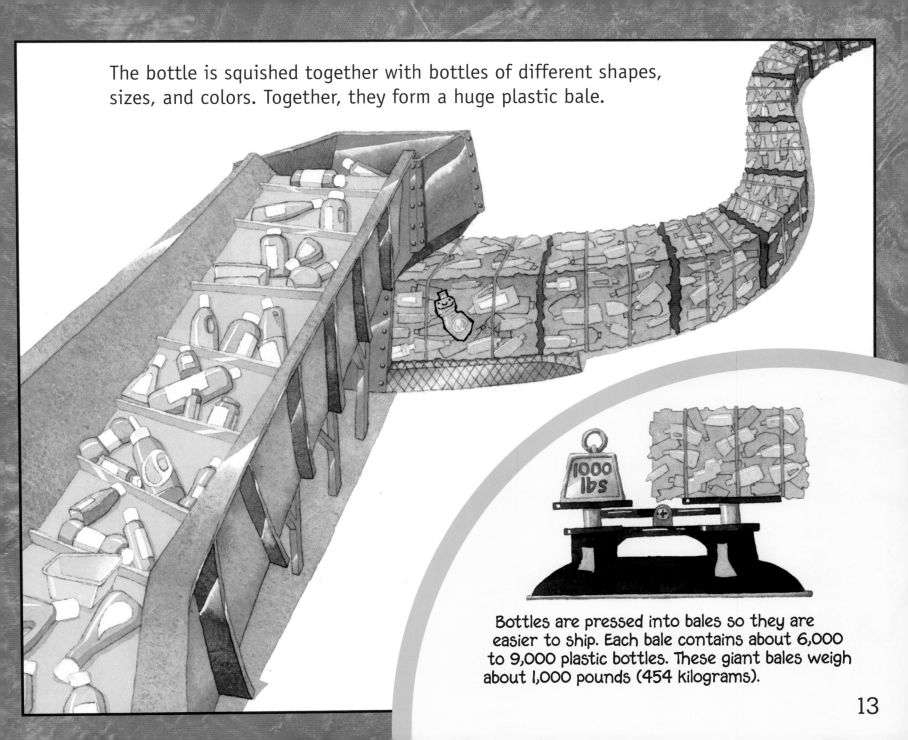

The bottle is squished together with bottles of different shapes, sizes, and colors. Together, they form a huge plastic bale.

Bottles are pressed into bales so they are easier to ship. Each bale contains about 6,000 to 9,000 plastic bottles. These giant bales weigh about 1,000 pounds (454 kilograms).

The bale takes a ride to a plastics reclaimer with many other bales.
There, it's busted apart, and the bottles are sorted by number.

The plastic bottle winds up with the number ones.

Number ones, over here!

I always knew I was number one.

Most plastic items have a number, 1 through 7, stamped on the bottom inside a triangle. The number shows the kind of pellets that were used to make the bottle. Numbers 1 and 2 are the most common types of bottles.

15

Chomp! Chomp! Chomp!

The plastic bottle is shredded inside a huge grinder.

16

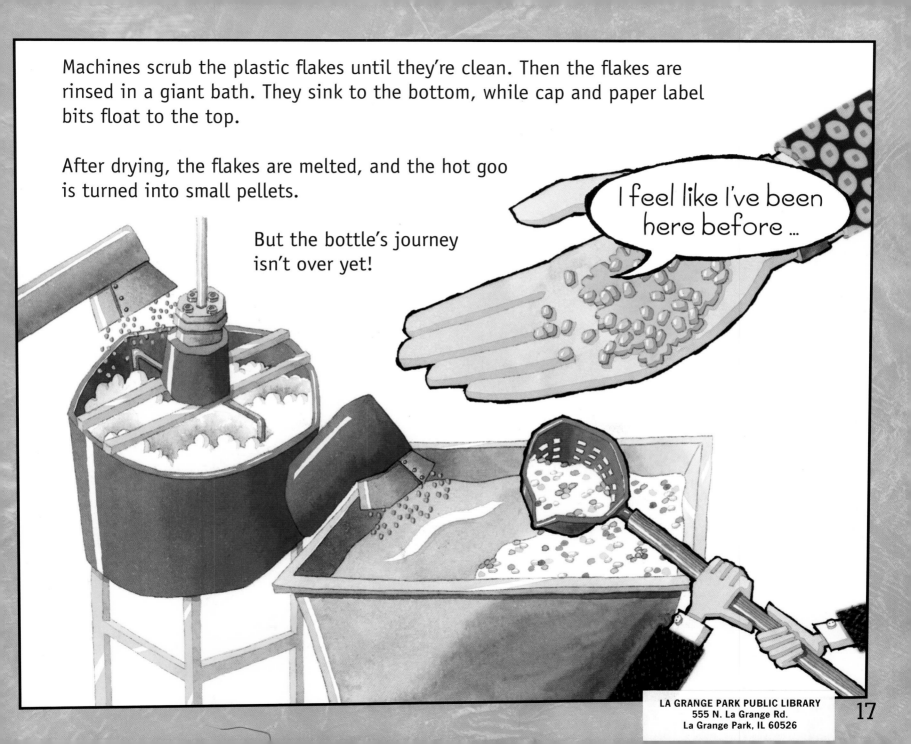

Machines scrub the plastic flakes until they're clean. Then the flakes are rinsed in a giant bath. They sink to the bottom, while cap and paper label bits float to the top.

After drying, the flakes are melted, and the hot goo is turned into small pellets.

But the bottle's journey isn't over yet!

I feel like I've been here before ...

The pellets travel to a factory, and the plastic bottle-making process begins again.

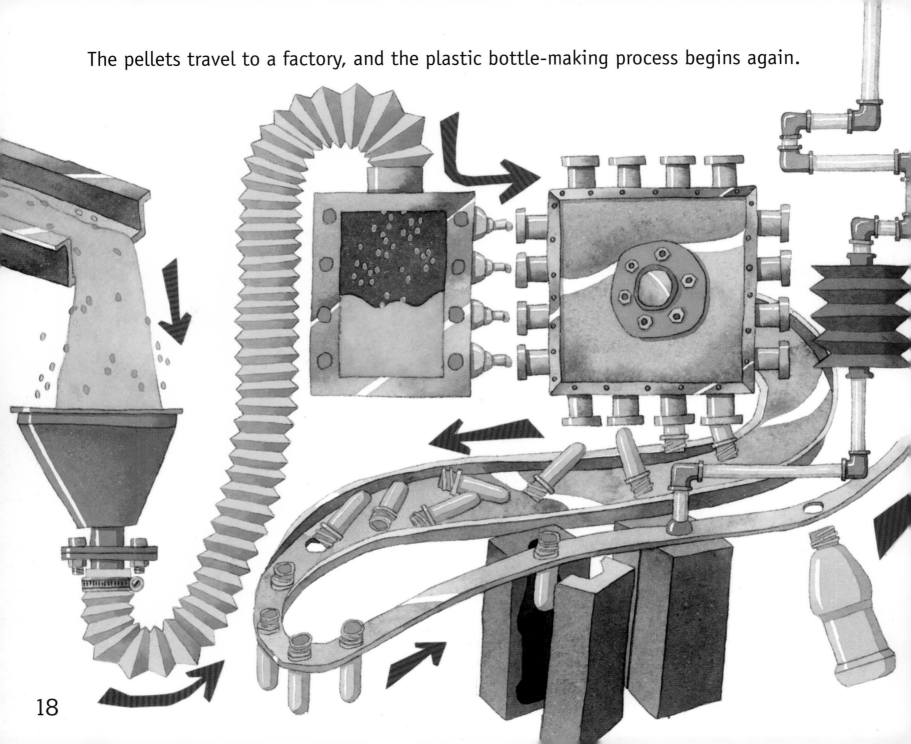

I LOVE the new me!

Recycled plastic bottles are turned into lots of new things besides bottles. Examples include carpet, park benches, fleece jackets, and fiberfill for coats and sleeping bags.

After being filled, capped, and labeled, the plastic bottle arrives at a grocery store. It doesn't sit long before a little girl grabs it.

This time, it's off to the soccer field!

Go, team!

In 2009, more than 2.4 billion pounds (1.1 billion kg) of plastic bottles were recycled into something new.

21

Diagram of a Plastic Bottle's Journey

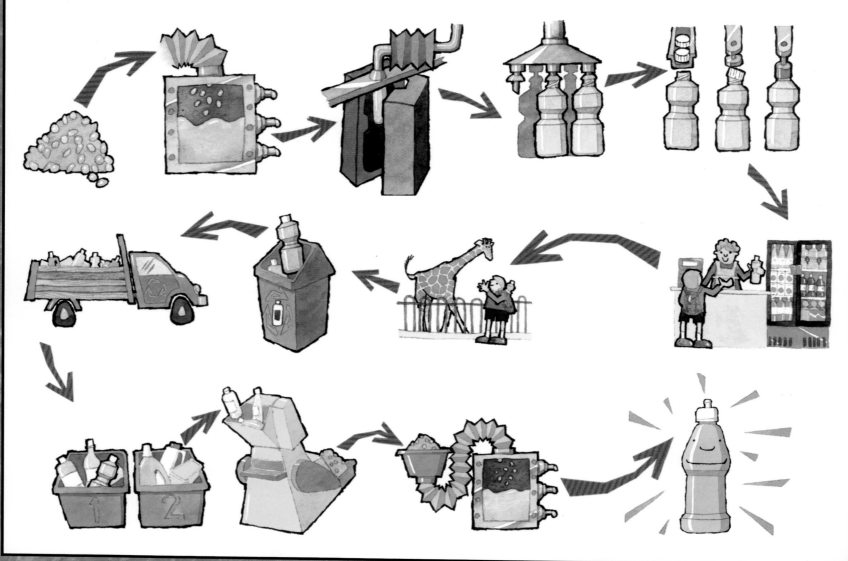

Glossary

bale—a large plastic brick made of thousands of plastic bottles squeezed together

pellet—a tiny piece of material made from petroleum or recycled plastics

plastics reclaimer—a place where plastic bottles are sorted by number and cleaned before they are made into pellets

recycle—to turn used goods, such as newspapers or soda cans, into new products

recycling facility—a place where used goods are baled for shipment to a reclaimer

To Learn More

More Books to Read

Fix, Alexandra. *Plastic.* Reduce, Reuse, Recycle. Chicago: Heinemann Library, 2008.

Inches, Alison. *The Adventures of a Plastic Bottle.* Little Green Books. New York: Little Simon, 2009.

Walker, Kate. *Plastic Bottles and Bags.* Recycling. New York: Marshall Cavendish Benchmark, 2011.

Internet Sites

FactHound offers a safe, fun way to find Internet sites related to this book. All of the sites on FactHound have been researched by our staff.

Here's all you do:
Visit *www.facthound.com*
Type in this code: 9781404862678

Super-cool stuff! Check out projects, games and lots more at
www.capstonekids.com

Index

Look for all the books in the Follow It series:

A Dollar Bill's Journey
A Germ's Journey

A Plastic Bottle's Journey
A Raindrop's Journey

CAPMOS DOG TRAINING

Safe and sound with child and dog

CADMOS

DOG TRAINING

Read
Learn
Know

Dagmar Cutka

Safe and sound with child and dog

CADMOS

Copyright © 2009 by Cadmos Verlag, Germany
Copyright of this edition © 2009 by Cadmos Books, Great Britain
Translation by Andrea Höfling
Layout and design: Grafikdesign Weber, Bremen
Cover photo: Christiane Slawik
All other photos: Christiane Slawik
Illustrations: Dr Eva Polsterer
Editorial of the original edition: Maren Müller
Editorial of this edition: Dr Sarah Binns, Christopher Long
Printed by: Westermann Druck, Zwickau

British Library Cataloguing in Publication Data
A catalogue record of this book is available from the British Library.

Printed in Germany
ISBN: 978-3-86127-971-6
www.cadmos.co.uk

Contents

*Together through
thick and thin.*

Introduction

'Child bitten by dog!' Again and again we see headlines such as these. What do we feel when we read them?

Do we feel sympathy with the child? Do we feel anger towards the dog? Or are we at a loss to understand the dog's owner? Do dogs really pose such a fundamental risk to children? Surely not! Unfortunately we usually only get to read about the negative events, when in fact we could fill volumes with the positive side of the story: 'Dog rescues child from drowning', 'Dog discovered child in the ruins of a house', 'Dog gets help when child falls and loses consciousness', to name but a few. Just think of the many dogs used for therapeutic purposes who perform unique tasks by supporting children with physical impairments in everyday life.

Children love dogs. They want to have a friend who will go through thick and thin with them, and to whom they can confide all their woes and their joys. Children and dogs enjoy the closeness they provide for each other, and through trust and love a friendship of a very special kind develops.

Children who grow up with dogs are more active and are happier to engage in social contact than other children. They learn early in life how to bear responsibility, and as a result improve their social skills. They suffer less from boredom, which makes them less likely to turn into TV or computer nerds. If it weren't for the negative headlines mentioned above, there would be plenty of good reasons for wanting to adopt a dog into the family, or at least to enable children to have contact with dogs.

How do these encounters between children and dogs that have a negative outcome arise in the first place? When dogs display aggressive behaviour towards children this may be the result of wrong or non-existent upbringing. On the other hand, accidents often happen because a dog feels threatened by a child who unwittingly engages in the 'wrong' behaviour. It doesn't have to be like this! In this book I want to demonstrate how you can playfully teach children how to interact with dogs in a safe manner. This could be the beginning of a great friendship between your dog and child!

A friend for life

'I'd really like to have a dog.' Almost every child wishes for a dog at some point in their life, and I was no exception. When I was eight years old, my parents fulfilled my wish, and a cute cocker spaniel puppy by the name of Sammy moved in with us. Sammy became my best friend who went with me everywhere and to whom I could entrust all my deepest feelings and thoughts. I enthusiastically helped to look after him, and after a while I came to understand his language better and better and was able to recognise when he needed something. As a side-effect, I learned how to take on responsibility and react to the needs of others.

If you want to grant your child's wish for a dog, first you should discuss this plan with the whole family. In order to prevent the project 'dog' from sinking without a trace before it even starts, all family members should be willing to share their future lives with 'man's best friend', and to take on some of the responsibility. Explain to your child that a dog is not a toy that you can put to one side when you're fed up with it, but a living being that needs daily care for many years to come. However, be aware as parents that you have to be part of the companionship between child and dog at all times. It is only with your help that your child is going to be able to learn to understand the dog's language and to recognise and respect the dog's needs. The child will learn to understand that they should not anthropomorphise their dog, while at the same time they should not become too dog-like. Nevertheless, to a large degree the dog's upbringing and care will remain your job – a child is not yet able take on these tasks alone. The child should be included and involved according to their age.

In spite of all this, your child will always see the dog first and foremost as a friend who is always there for them, with whom they can play and have fun – and provided that their dealings with each other are guided by mutual respect, this is just fine.

Is there such a thing as the ideal dog for children?

It would be better to ask: 'How do I encourage a dog to become child-friendly?' No dog is born an ideal dog for children, but every dog can learn to like children. What makes a dog a loving companion for your child

Children can help to care for a dog from an early age.

No matter how cute the dog may be, as a family you ought to give some thought to whether they really are compatible with your family.

does not depend on the breed, but rather on whether the dog has been used to interacting with children from an early age, and whether the dog has had any negative prior experiences with them.

What type of dog is most suitable for our family?

This doesn't mean that it doesn't matter what kind of dog is going to move in with you. Sit down together with the whole family and think about which breeds are worth

considering. Take your time when choosing a dog and don't be guided by the dog's outward appearance. On no account buy a dog because your child thinks he's cute. Children in particular often tend to go for so-called 'fashion dogs'. Just bear in mind that even dogs such as golden retrievers aren't born as loving child-friendly dogs. They have to be brought up accordingly, and have to get used to children just like any other dog. Make every effort to find out what tasks your preferred breed has originally been bred to perform, because each breed has very specific traits and needs. This also applies to mixed-breed dogs, who show an amalgamation of the traits of several breeds. Think very carefully whether the dog is compatible with your lifestyle and your children, and whether you'll be able to keep them occupied in a manner appropriate for their species, in order to provide the dog with sufficient mental and physical challenges.

When you choose a suitable breed or a mixed-breed dog, it doesn't matter whether you or your family already have experience with dogs, or whether this will be your first dog.

However, if the latter is the case you should plump for a representative of a breed that is known for being relatively easy to bring up.

 Tip

When choosing your family dog you should make sure that your desired breed has a high stimulation threshold, and is not known to be nervous or sensitive to noise.

You have to make a fundamental decision about whether you want to raise a puppy, or if you'd rather offer a home to an older dog. If you go for a puppy, please make sure you go to a responsible breeder. Among other things, you'll recognise a good breeder by the fact that all their dogs live in the house, and not in a kennel. In this way the puppies get used to a variety of things from an early age that they're likely to encounter in everyday life. Visit several breeders with

your child, and don't be shy about asking any questions that come to mind. In particular ask about what socialisation with children the puppies have had up to now. In the best case scenario the puppies are already living with children in the breeder's family, and are able to gain positive experiences with them from day one.

If you'd rather take in an older dog, again you should look into the matter very closely. Great care has to be taken, especially with dogs from a rescue home, because there will be many difficult dogs, and dogs whose previous history is unknown, who are waiting there for a new home. Get some reliable information, and be sure to take your child with you. Take the dog you might like to have for a little walk to see how they react to your child. By doing so you preempt potential problems that may otherwise only manifest themselves once you're back home with the family, and you also spare the dog the pain of being returned to the rescue home.

Do you want a small dog, a medium-sized dog, or a large dog? Whether the dog is large or small, every dog has to be brought up with consistency and has to be kept sufficiently occupied, both mentally and physically. However, small dogs are often more insecure than large dogs, and can feel cornered or threatened by a child, because even a toddler is considerably larger than they are.

Please also spare a thought for the texture of your new housemate's fur. Are you able to put up with dog hairs scattered around the whole house, or would you prefer a breed that sheds few hairs? How much time do you want to invest in grooming the dog? Long-haired dogs have to be brushed daily, and some breeds require a haircut on a regular basis.

All the above-mentioned tips can only provide you with a few clues; any more information would exceed the remit of this book. You will find tips for further reading in the Appendix which you might find useful in your quest for a suitable dog.

How to make a dog child-friendly

The socialisation of a dog begins at birth. As described in the previous chapter, the foundation for child-friendliness is laid by the breeder. Once the new family member has moved in with you, you take over the responsibility for their further development.

At the beginning allow the newcomer some peace and quiet, and don't confront them with too many things at once. On the first day your child should only greet the dog briefly, and not claim the dog for themselves the whole time. This should remain the case for the next few days as well. After about one week you can begin to introduce the little dog to other children of all ages and backgrounds. However, this has to be done calmly and gradually. If there are too many children homing in on a little puppy at once, who will all want to stroke it and pick it up, the puppy is put under far too much stress, and it is possible that in future they may want to avoid children altogether as a result.

During these first few days it is likely that your child will want to show off their puppy proudly to their friends. You will have to dampen this enthusiasm a little: the best way is to invite only one friend at a time. This enables the puppy to make contact with the (to the puppy) unknown child without undue stress.

 Tip

Please don't confront the puppy with a different child every day, but allow a few days between child visitors to give them an opportunity to relax.

Always keep an eye on the children and the dog, in order to be able to intervene quickly if necessary. In the first weeks and months any potentially bad experiences the puppy may have with children should be avoided at all costs. The trust of the puppy towards children would be destroyed, and it would take a long time and a lot of patience for it to be restored.

You should certainly take immediate action to inhibit puppy´s biting response. Young dogs don't know from birth how much force they may apply with their teeth when playing with other dogs or humans. They learn through trial and error how much force is acceptable when biting. Your puppy has already been 'trained' in bite inhibition in their first weeks with their littermates, and you have to continue this training. If a puppy bites too firmly during play with their littermates, their playing partner will scream and break off the game. This way the rude puppy learns that biting too firmly ends the nice game, and they will be more cautious in the future. The same applies

This is all right. The puppy touches the child gently just with his lips and tongue.

to playing with humans: if the little chap becomes too rough, play is immediately interrupted. Your puppy is only allowed to touch your child with their lips or tongue, and not with their teeth.

Even for older dogs who have missed out on socialisation with children it is still possible to do some catching up. This, however, requires a lot of time, patience and experience. In this case, as with all behavioural problems, you must ask the advice of an expert dog trainer.

 Important

If you are unsure whether your dog is able to cope in a certain situation, try to put yourself in their place and listen to your inner voice. If your inner sense tells you that the dog has had enough, or even feels uncomfortable, you should not allow it to go on. Only if you accept the dog's needs, and don't ask too much of them will they be able to develop into a canine companion for your child who is friendly and has strength of character. A dog who is always forced to endure anything that is thrown at them will not become child-friendly.

The dog was the number one in your life up to now. If you prepare them properly they will have no problem sharing your attention with a baby.

If the dog was there first

So you already have a dog, and now you're expecting a baby? Then you should prepare your dog for the newcomer during the pregnancy. Up to now your dog was the number one, and they have gradually got to learn that soon they will have to share you with somebody else. If you convey this to your dog in an agreeable manner, nothing should stand in the way of a harmonious co-existence of baby and dog. However, this is only true on the condition that your dog has no problems with children generally. Should this not be the case you must work together with an expert in dog behaviour.

To practise you need a doll and some really tasty treats. Carry the doll around with you, sit it on the sofa or on the floor and let your dog sniff it – they will be curious and will want to know what you've got in your arms. Whenever they approach the 'baby' gently and cautiously, reward the dog with a treat. Take the doll in your arms every time you feed the dog as well. In this way the dog will associate the doll with positive things and you can practise everyday life with baby and dog as you go along.

If you have friends who happen to have a baby, it is a good idea to invite them to your home, or to visit them with the dog, so the dog can get used to the smell of a baby. Busy yourself with the baby, take it in your arms, but stroke or feed the dog at the same time. If your dog is excited and tries to jump up at you, put them on the leash for a few minutes until they have calmed down. Don't forget to praise the dog for approaching the baby in a friendly and cautious manner.

Record a CD of baby crying noises that you can play from time to time in your home in order to make this a familiar everyday sound for your dog, so they won't be startled by it every time. As soon as you have your pram at home, take it with you on your walks. The dog will quickly get used to the large thing on wheels, and at the same time you can practise the simultaneous handling of dog and pram.

 Important
Never tie the leash to the pram. Even the most well-behaved dog will occasionally pull on the leash and this could make the pram topple over.

Decide whether or not the future nursery will be taboo for the dog. If yes, you should establish the taboo zone now, so the dog already accepts the door to this room as a border by the time the baby moves in. It is nicer for the dog, however, if they are allowed to be part of things in here too. If this is the case, you ought to teach your dog to leave the room at your request.

 Tip
Leaving a room can be trained using the same method as that described for asking the dog to get off the sofa in the chapter 'Life with children and dogs'.

Secure the room with a child safety gate so your dog doesn't feel excluded if they are not allowed in once in a while. The safety gate will be useful later when the baby is crawling. You can use it to separate dog and child from each other in order to allow the dog to enjoy resting periods undisturbed.

Once the happy event has come to pass, and mother and baby are spending the first few days in hospital, dad can bring home a used nappy and a worn romper-suit for the dog. The dog should be allowed to sniff these items thoroughly, for which they will receive enthusiastic praise. When mother and baby return home the dog will recognise the smell of the newborn, and will already have made a positive association with it.

Your dog will have missed their mistress, and will be even more pleased when the family is complete again. Give them time and the opportunity for a thorough welcome. Dad and baby can wait outside for a bit, and follow mum indoors a few minutes later. The dog should then be allowed to greet the baby too. For this you hold the baby at the dog's eye level and let them sniff the baby thoroughly. Please don't forget to praise and cuddle the dog.

Now the real stress of parenting can begin. The situation isn't just new for your dog, but also for yourselves. The everyday routines with the baby have yet to be established. Don't feel guilty if you shunt your dog's habitual time slots for feeding and going for walks around a little. They will forgive you for seeing to their needs belatedly if you do it in a relaxed manner, rather than feeding the dog in a hurried manner or only taking them for a very quick walk.

 Important
Don't neglect your dog. Reserve some playing and cuddling time for them, when you

can dedicate yourself to the dog alone, so the problem of jealously doesn't arise in the first place. Have the dog participate in everything you do with the child, and reward every positive behaviour.

Now the time has arrived for baby visitors. This is very exciting for the dog. They should always be allowed to be present, so these visits will be normal and part of every-day life, and so they will at no point come to believe that they have to protect the baby from strangers.

When your baby begins to crawl you will not just have to keep an eye on the child, but you will also have to protect the dog from the child. Make sure from the outset that the dog is left in peace, and intervene immediately if you notice that the dog is feeling pestered. You must keep the child away from the dog's sleeping place, and their food bowl and toys.

 Important
No matter how friendly and gentle your dog is – don't ever leave them alone in a room with your baby.

The language of children

Children are impulsive little people who express their moods not just in a verbal form but also consciously or subconsciously through their body language. Especially with small children, tempers sometimes get out of hand. In this situation they no longer have any regard for others, whether they are humans or dogs. When children are pleased or excited they run around the house squealing and thumping; if they don't get their way, they can throw tantrums, screaming and stomping their feet, sometimes a toy goes flying across the sitting room as well. Things can get particularly boisterous when there are other children visiting.

A dog can feel threatened by the behaviours described above, especially by the uncontrolled body language. In these situations you have to intervene decisively in order to protect the dog, but also the child or children. Things can get dangerous if the dog tries to defend itself, or if during a quarrel between your child and a strange child the dog takes the side of their 'pack member'.

 Important
Never leave child and dog unsupervised! The impulsive body language of children can appear threatening to dogs and prompt them to react in a defensive manner.

Please don't blame your children for their behaviour. They don't yet know that the dog

Quarrelling children are often loud and their body language is uncontrolled. This can make a dog feel very insecure.

perceives it as unpleasant. Although dogs indicate clearly when they're feeling uneasy, children have to learn to pay attention to the dog's language, interpret the warning signals correctly, and react accordingly. For this they first have to become conscious of their own body language, and understand what effect it has on dogs.

Learning game

This game demonstrates to children what effect a heavy quarrel has on a dog. There should be three children involved.

Two children simulate a quarrel involving loud words and fisticuffs – they should of course not really hurt each other. The third child observes how the dog re-acts to the quarrel, and memorises what they have seen. (They can also write it down together.) Then the children swap roles, and when each of them in turn has observed the dog, you should sit down with all of them and encourage them to discuss their observations. The children will probably have noticed that the dog has not exactly felt happy and relaxed during these quarrels, and they themselves will have experienced similar uneasiness during their stint as observer.

After the game all the children have probably realised that a quarrel can be very unpleasant to observe, for humans and animals alike.

The language of dogs

Among themselves dogs rarely communicate using sound language, but rather with their body language. When interacting with human beings, dogs also mainly use the signals of their body language. Dogs express themselves more clearly and use audible signals such as growling and barking only when humans are unable to read their body language signals, or don't react to them.

In order to be able to understand our own dog better, and strange dogs too, we humans have to learn to read the language of dogs. Then we will be able to recognise whether a situation is pleasant or unpleasant for the dog, whether they are in a good mood and perhaps keen to play, or whether they are scared or potentially feeling threatened.

 Important

Dangerous situations and accidents can be avoided if your child is able to recognise whether a dog is scared or in a threatening mode, and if they know that in this case they have to keep well away from the dog. Any move in the direction of the dog is interpreted as a threat. The right thing for the child to do is to turn and walk slowly away.

This is quite difficult, particularly for small children, but even they are already able to recognise some very clear signals. The easiest feature to judge is the position of the tail, because with most dogs the tail movement can be seen quite clearly. The ear movement is a little trickier to assess, especially with floppy-eared dogs.

In order to be able to interpret the body language properly you should never rely on just one signal. You always have to look at the entire dog. Only when looking at the whole picture, i.e. tail position, ear movement and facial expression, can you get an idea about what's going on inside the animal's mind. It is important for your child to know this and to learn to interpret various combinations of these signals, and to show consideration for the dog's needs accordingly.

With the help of the drawings in the following section that show the signals of the dog's body language you can show your child what a dog looks like when it is feeling relaxed and secure, when it is offering an invitation to play, and when it is scared or in a threatening mode.

 Important

Many parents and children think that a dog who is wagging its tail is always a friendly dog. Caution, this is a grave error! If the dog wags its tail at great speed, usually with its whole backside also in motion, this does mean the dog is in a friendly mood. If a dog feels threatened or is itself in a threatening mode, it wags its tail slowly, almost twitching, while displaying a tense and stiff body posture.

Important body language signals

Secure and relaxed

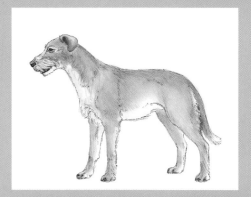

When a dog is feeling relaxed, their body posture is erect and their movements appear calm and harmonious. The dog's muscles are relaxed, with the tail hanging down loosely.

The mouth is either closed or slightly open, the lips are relaxed. The ears are in their natural position. It is a friendly expression.

Invitation to play

If a dog wants to play they will often indicate this by adopting the bowing position – an invitation to play that is characteristic of dogs. The chest and the front legs, including the elbows, touch the ground, the rear end points upwards. If a dog jumps around boisterously while wagging their tail strongly, so their whole rear end moves about, they are also in a playful mood.

The mouth is slightly open, the corners of the mouth are pulled back and slightly upwards, the whole facial expression is friendly. Sometimes dogs in a playful mood bark briefly and excitedly, with a high pitch.

Fear

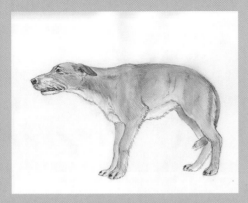

If a dog is feeling insecure or is scared, their whole body is tense, the hind legs are slightly bent and the back is rounded. The dog cowers and their head is lowered. The tail hangs low, sometimes clinched between the legs.

The ears are pinned back close to the head, their tips pointing towards the spine. The corners of the mouth are pulled backwards, to reveal the tips of the teeth. The eyes are wide open, but may appear narrower because of the whole facial area being pulled backwards.

Posturing and the threatening stance

In order to assume a threatening stance, a dog tenses their muscles and their movements appear stiff and tense. The tail points backwards horizontally, or almost vertically upwards; in addition some dogs will move their tail back and forth. The hairs on the neck and back stand on end, similar to a brush, i.e. the hackles are raised.

The ears are upright (with floppy-eared dogs this is not very obvious, only slightly visible at the root of the ear) and are pointing forwards. The dog fixes their opponent with their eyes. In order to emphasise the threatening stance the dog pulls up their lips to reveal the front teeth and canines. Often the threatening stance is reinforced by a growl.

Learning game

This observation game helps children to learn to understand the dog's body language. You can play this game with several children.

Everybody sits around a table and waits until things have quietened down, and the dog appears to be relaxed and happy. Then everyone is given the task of accurately describing the expression of the dog's eyes and lips, and the position of their ears and tail. The children can also draw pictures of what they see. In this way they learn what a relaxed dog looks like. Later on this will help them to recognise changes, such as the expression of excitement or anxiety, that indicate that the dog isn't feeling very much at ease right now. The children will soon enjoy observing the dog's body posture at every opportunity, and working out what it may mean.

They can copy the drawings from this book as well, in order to practise observing body posture and facial expressions. Show your child each picture and have them explain to you what the dog in the picture is trying to say, and from which part of the body the child has been able to tell this first. Alternatively, your child could compare a specific part of the body, for example the tail, in all the different situations pictured. How does the dog hold his tail when he is relaxed, as opposed to when he is scared?

These games give children a greater understanding of dogs, and with it more confidence in dealing with them on a daily basis.

If a dog is licking its nose it is feeling uneasy. On the photo this is easy to see; in reality it happens so fast that children don't usually notice it.

Early warning signals

If a dog feels disturbed by a child, or the playing and stroking has got a bit much for them, they will express this by using the same subtle signals they would use when dealing with other dogs – and they will do this long before they begin to behave in an openly threatening manner, as demonstrated in the previous section. The dog will lick their nose and fangs with their tongue, yawn, scratch, and turn their head away. Only if these warning signals aren't being respected will the dog pull back their lips, growl or snap in the direction of the child. After all, a dog doesn't have a pair of hands to push the child away, and a dog isn't able to say that they want the child to stop. A dog has only its teeth to defend itself with.

Because children are not yet capable of recognising a dog's initial warning signals, it is up to you to keep an eye on child and

The head is turned away: the husky is feeling uncomfortable in this situation, and he demonstrates this quite clearly by turning his head away from you.

Baring of teeth and growling: this clear threat is only deployed when all previous signals have been ignored.

dog, and to ensure that the dog is left in peace as soon as they indicate that they are no longer feeling at ease.

 Important

Don't ever forbid your dog to growl, because this would effectively forbid them sending out a warning signal. As a consequence the dog may end up biting without warning when they are feeling cornered.

Observe child and dog closely and intervene early, before your dog feels obliged to issue a clear warning.

 Real life dog stories

A family asked my advice: after their male dog, named Ares, had snapped at one of the children without warning, slightly injuring him. The family considered getting rid of the dog, fearing that worse was to come. During a counselling session it turned out that Ares had been punished every time he had growled at the children. Thus he had effectively been banned from issuing a warning, and as a result he saw no other way of dealing with a disagreeable situation than to snap straight away.

Now all the family members are learning to observe Ares more closely, to recognise early warning signals and to respect them. Through patient training, Ares has been turned back into the friendly playmate for the children he had been before.

This is how it's meant to be: harmony and agreement among children and dogs.

Life with children and dogs

Children and dogs have a lot in common: dogs live in the here and now, as do children. Dogs are selfish, so are children. Both deploy various strategies in order to get what they want, and both need rules that help them to find their way and to distinguish between right and wrong behaviour. Therefore you should establish clear rules with regard to child and dog sharing their lives together. Don't let advice from well-meaning friends and acquaintances, or perhaps from dog trainers, make you feel unsure about yourself. You and your family have the final say about what child and dog are allowed to do.

Importantly, however, the rules should always serve the best interest and safety of all involved, and they should be adhered to consistently by every family member from the outset. It is quite common for a dog to enjoy many freedoms while they are a cute little puppy, only to have these taken away when they have grown up.

This is exactly the sort of situation that a dog doesn't understand any more than a child would: why all of a sudden are they supposed to sleep in their own bed, when they were warmly welcomed into their parents´ bed during infancy, just because they have grown older and bigger?

Sit down with your child, and think together about which rules should apply to the dog and which rules to the child. Establishing taboos is also part of this process. Some are strictly necessary for safety reasons – for example, food in a child's hands should always be taboo for a dog.

Other taboos depend on the needs of the child. Some children don't mind if the dog plays with their toys, others don't like it at all. In the latter case one of the rules could state that the children's toys are taboo for the dog.

Once children and dogs learn to show consideration towards each other, nothing can stand in the way of a wonderful friendship.

Tip
Write down the rules for child and dog, or, if you have a smaller child, draw a picture with them, which you hang up for all to see, for example in the kitchen. This gives the child the opportunity to check in case they have forgotten one of the rules.

Health rules

Some parasites and canine diseases can be passed on to humans. In order to prevent this you have to de-worm your dog on a regular basis and have the vet vaccinate them regularly.

Very small children are not able to grasp the concept of hygiene. They are curious, touch everything and often stick their fingers into their mouths afterwards. If your dog is allowed to do their business in the garden, always remember to remove the faeces immediately and thoroughly. Washing hands after stroking and cuddling the dog should become routine for your child.

Is the dog allowed on the sofa or the bed?

Preventing the dog from taking a higher ranking position to that of the human is still a common recommendation. Many dog experts still advise you not to allow the dog on the sofa or the bed under any circumstances, because by occupying these places the dog seeks to strengthen their position in the family hierarchy. However, nowadays there are just as many experts who are of a different opinion. Dogs like to lie on the sofa or on the bed, because these are comfortable places to lie down on, nothing more!

Zeus's favourite spot is the sofa. This is all right, as long as he will give it up again on command.

Zeus instantly reacts to Marlies' command and gets off the sofa.

Children feel more secure with a dog by their side, and love it if they spend the night together. And why not! I personally don't see anything reprehensible in this. However, for reasons of hygiene it is not advisable for the dog to slip under the covers with your child.

Instead put a blanket at the bottom of the bed where the dog can make itself comfortable.

Of course it is entirely up to you whether your dog is allowed on the sofa or the bed. If these places are out of bounds to the dog right from the outset, they will be content with a basket or a blanket on the floor.

 Tip

If you don't mind dog hairs on the furniture, you can cuddle up with child and dog on the sofa without a guilty conscience. For dogs, a sofa is nothing more than a comfy place to relax!

If a dog defends their comfortable place on the sofa or the bed, this doesn't represent a dominance behaviour, but rather it is due to the fact that the dog hasn't learnt to give up their cosy spot upon your signal. Therefore teach the dog that they have to leave the sofa or the bed at any given time without hesitation or grumbling whenever you ask them to, and have your child practise this under your supervision as well.

This is how it's done:

Prepare a few treats and lure the dog on to the sofa. As soon as the dog has jumped up, take the treats in your hand and then guide your hand in a semicircular movement away from the dog towards the floor. Briefly look at your dog while you're doing this, and then look on to the floor to make sure the dog understands who you're talking to, and where they are supposed to go. The instant your dog climbs off the sofa, you say 'Off!', and once all four paws have touched the ground the dog gets a treat as a reward. By practising with a treat the dog is positively reinforced in his action, and doesn't feel displaced from their chosen spot. Repeat this exercise until the dog leaves the sofa without hesitation as soon as the signal 'Off!' is given. Include your child in this training session as well.

If the dog reacts reliably to your signal, you can practise it in everyday situations too. Wait until your dog has made themselves comfortable on the sofa unprompted. Take a treat and ask them to get off the sofa again, just as you have practised beforehand.

As soon as the dog obeys your signal reliably in everyday situations as well, you can omit the treat. Stay on the ball with this, nevertheless, and keep asking your dog at random intervals to get off the sofa – even if it isn't actually necessary – so they don't forget this important exercise.

Approaching the dog

Dogs with sound social behaviour patterns will avoid any frontal contact when they encounter fellow dogs. In order to avoid any conflict from the outset they display appeasement signals such as sniffing the head or the neck of the other dog, walking around them in a semi-circle, and averting their gaze.

Dogs are always polite upon meeting each other. Children should learn from them.

When children come across a dog, they often run impulsively towards it, often screaming and shouting, and stretch their arms out towards the dog. For a dog this is rather frightening behaviour and they will see only one option: flight! Children often don't understand this signal correctly. Instead of leaving the dog alone, they pursue them noisily, because they want to catch and stroke them. This can lead to a dog feeling cornered, leaving them no way of escape – a dangerous situation that you should never allow to arise in the first place. This is the reason why children have to learn how to approach a dog properly. They can learn a lot from dogs as far as the politeness of canine greet-ing rituals is concerned.

This is how it works:
Explain to the child how they should approach a dog correctly: always move slowly and calmly, approaching the dog from the side in a semicircle. Not from the front, not too fast, and under no circumstances from be-hind, because if the dog notices the child too late they may get startled. However, it would be best for the child not to approach the dog at all, but to sit on the ground instead, and let the dog decide for itself whether or not to establish contact. If the dog is not pestered they will almost invariably be happy to ac-cept the child's invitation and run towards the child.

Proper stroking

Dogs are living beings with emotions and feelings; children forget this all too easily and should be reminded, if necessary.

 Important
If your child pinches the dog on purpose or pulls their tail or ears, jealousy could

This child knows that he should never pester a dog. He waits patiently until the greyhound establishes friendly contact of his own accord.

be at the bottom of this behaviour. Maybe your child feels that you are paying the dog too much attention. Try to divide your attention evenly between child and dog, and always involve your child in everything to do with the dog.

Small children in particular are often rough in the way they touch dogs because they don't yet possess the necessary fine motor skills for gentle touches. You should therefore practise tenderly stroking the dog, so as not to hurt them. Show the child how and where the dog likes to be stroked.

Dogs particularly like being stroked behind the ears, on the neck and on the tummy. You don't need to apply any pressure because dogs are very sensitive. They are able to sense a fly landing on their fur. Being touched too firmly may feel rather unpleasant to them. Something dogs really dislike is having their head stroked from above, and being slapped on their side or patted on the head.

Often dogs don't want to be stroked at all. They simply aren't in the mood for this and show this clearly by walking away from the child. This always has to be accepted by the child. They must leave the dog alone, and not pester the dog with well-intentioned tokens of their love and fondness.

This is how it's done:
Take the child's hand and use it to gently stroke their own cheeks. Then have the child try the same thing by themselves. This way your child will develop a feeling for the degree of gentleness they should employ when stroking the dog.

You can also show older children how to pamper the dog with a massage. Most dogs enjoy this form of stroking very much after they have had a fulfilled or exciting day. The dog should be lying on its side and be relaxed. In order to get a dog to lie on its side, first have them assume the 'sit' position. Now take a treat in your hand and guide it from the dog's nose towards their back, until the dog drops on to its side in order to reach the treat.

Now the massage can begin. The child starts on the neck and strokes the dog's fur along the back up to the root of the tail, gently and without applying pressure. Then, using slow and even movements, the child works their way towards the tummy, where dogs like to be stroked most of all. After a while the dog is carefully turned over to the other side and massaged there in the same fashion. As before, this works best with the help of a treat.

The first few times the whole massage should be a short affair to give the dog a chance to get used to it. Later, if you notice that your dog is enjoying the interaction, your child can gradually increase the massage time, to a maximum of twenty minutes.

Even small children can learn how to stroke a dog tenderly.

Real life dog stories

A family and their nine-week-old mixed-breed dog Nero took part in one of my puppy classes. They brought their three-year-old son along with them. I was horrified to see how the little boy treated the dog. He hit Nero on the head with his palm, kicked him, and then again he hugged him tightly, almost choking the dog. The parents didn't intervene. I demonstrated to them during an individual training session how to teach their son to treat the dog respectfully. Unfortunately neither the parents' nor their son's behaviour changed. The parents couldn't cope at all with the situation, and we came to the joint conclusion that the best solution would be to find a new home for Nero. Unfortunately this is a rather sad aspect of my work.

Picking up and carrying

Children love to pick up puppies and carry them around, but will also do the same to small adult dogs. As a rule you should not permit this, because most dogs feel extremely uncomfortable when they haven't got all four paws on the ground.

Of course there are always situations where a dog ought to be carried. If you have a puppy of only a few months old it is important to carry them up the stairs and to lift them in or out of the car in order to avoid putting the still soft joints under too much stress. If your child is physically capable of doing this, and there is no risk of them losing their balance with the dog in their arms, they should be able to undertake this task. How-ever, you have to show the child exactly how to pick up and carry a dog properly without hurting or injuring them.

This is how it's done:
Your child stands next to the dog's side, and puts one hand under the chest and the other hand around the rear end of the dog. Now the child can lift the dog. Please ensure that your child puts the dog down carefully and gently afterwards.

When the dog is eating

Many dog care manuals still advise you to take away the food bowl from a dog while it's eating, and then to put it back straight away. This is supposed to demonstrate to the dog that the human is above them in the hierarchy, and is therefore allowed to approach the bowl at any time and to take away the food. The jury is still out on wheth-er this message is completely lost on the dog anyway. The dog will probably learn to wolf down the food quickly in order to have it finished by the time you take it away again. Eating is important to a dog, and the fear of not getting enough means stress – which leads to indigestion and

While Marlies is holding her hand in a horizontal position, Zeus has to wait.

Even if the food bowl is already in place.

behavioural problems. As a consequence a dog may defend its food aggressively.

For this reason you should ensure that your dog is able to have their meal in peace. While the dog is eating children should under no circumstances stroke the dog, nor put their hand into the food bowl. However, don't feed the dog in a separate room out of misplaced consideration, because this would only isolate them. A dog is far happier eating its food in the presence of the family.

It is best to feed the dog before you have your own meals. Provided that none of the family members secretly passes food to the dog under the table, doing things in this order prevents begging at the table, because the dog will no longer be hungry by the time the family is eating. Have your child help you prepare the dog food, and let them put the food bowl in front of the dog. The dog should have

learned already that they must wait quietly until the bowl has been put in its place, and that they are only allowed to eat once the command has been given. This prevents the dog jumping up at the child in order to reach their food.

This is how it's done:

Your child takes the filled food bowl and stands upright next to the food stand or mat. The child waits there until the dog sits down without a command. As soon as the dog has sat down, they receive praise. Next the child places the bowl in the stand or on the mat while giving the dog a waiting signal which stops the dog from getting to the bowl. For example the child can hold an open hand in front of the dog's nose. The dog is only allowed to start eating when a release signal has been given.

At the beginning the interval between the waiting signal and the release signal has to

Marlies gives the release signal. Now Zeus is allowed to eat.

Please do not disturb!

When a dog is living with children, things can get a bit turbulent at times. That's why periods of peace and quiet are especially important to a dog. Particularly after eating and after playing sessions with your child, you should permit the dog to take a break. Set up a cosy refuge for your dog where they can get away from the hurly-burly of family life. The best place would be somewhere people rarely pass through and where there is no danger that the dog may be trodden on.

If the dog goes to their sleeping place of their own accord, this is a clear indication that they don't want to be disturbed. Should your child approach the dog nevertheless, the dog will signal their need for rest by turning their head away, and if that doesn't lead to success, the dog will possibly growl and snap into the air. Don't scold your dog for doing so. The dog is not attacking the child, this is only their way of saying, 'Go away and leave me in peace!' A dog has no other way of making itself understood.

Let sleeping dogs lie! Children are well advised to take this rule seriously. It would be best to declare the dog's resting place an absolute taboo zone for your child. This is because a dog who has to fend off unwanted advances again and again will at some point begin to defend their refuge in earnest.

Your child should never stroke or pick up a sleeping dog from their resting place, or any other place. The dog may get startled to the degree that they might suddenly snap at the child.

be rather brief, because the dog has still to learn how to wait.

Once the dog has understood what they are supposed to do, the interval can be extended. In the case of smaller children you should give the waiting and release signals yourself. This gives your child the opportunity to concentrate on handling the food bowl.

Tip

If your child is old enough to perform this task you can ask them to ensure that the dog always has a supply of fresh water. By doing this the child learns to take some responsibility for the dog.

Please still keep an eye on the water bowl to prevent your dog from having to go thirsty if your child forgets to replenish the supply.

Real life dog stories

Recently a family asked for my help. Their one-year-old mixed-breed dog Jack was very nervous, and he avoided their four-year-old son.

First of all I observed the child and the dog. No matter where Jack went in order to retreat, the boy always followed him, pestering and squeezing him. Jack growled at the boy as soon as he approached him. He was obviously annoyed by the child's behaviour.

I advised the parents to make sure that Jack was always allowed to enjoy his rest periods without being disturbed. When I visited the family a second time, Jack was playing with the boy in a relaxed and happy manner.

Please do not disturb! The beagle Akira has retreated to her cosy little spot.

The dog's education

Children enjoy emulating adults. When they see that a dog is following instructions, they want to be able to give instructions to the dog themselves. Don't hesitate to involve your child in your dog's education. Later on the dog will obey not only you, but also your child. Bear in mind, however, that in most cases this will work only at home in familiar surroundings, where the dog isn't being distracted by environmental stimuli.

If you're venturing out of doors, the dog will probably obey only you. For dogs, children are generally playmates of equal status, and they are rarely accepted as leaders.

Have the child watch you during training sessions and involve them where possible. Practise this sequence as a dry run first, i.e. without the dog, to enable your child to gain confidence. When the child takes on the role of dog trainer later – under your supervision – they can concentrate fully on the dog, and will know exactly what to do. This is of particular importance, because an insecure child who isn't sufficiently familiar with the exercise sequence will speak their own body language. The dog will not understand what is expected of them, and as a consequence won't carry out the exercise. This will be greatly disappointing to the child.

Make sure you pay attention to the tone of your voice. If your voice sounds severe and loud when you give commands to the dog, your child will talk to the dog in a commanding voice as well. They will take their cue from you. Always bear in mind that for dogs, everything we teach them is a trick, and tricks are practised with a calm, friendly voice, a lot of patience and a smile on your face. This also applies to exercises such as 'sit' and 'down'.

We humans may attach great importance to these two commands, but for dogs they are no more and no less important than 'hand-shake' or 'stand up on your hind legs'. Your dog will reward you and your child for your kindness, calmness and patience during these training sessions with their enthusiastic cooperation.

 Important
Please don't forget that dogs, like children, need periods of rest between learning sessions. Always keep the sessions short to avoid putting your dog under too much pressure. The best moment for ending an exercise is when the dog is doing

particularly well. As a result they will join in happily next time.

Children from the age of twelve years onwards can practise with the dog unsupervised, on the condition that you are sure that the child will treat the animal with kindness and respect. Younger children should not be left on their own during training sessions. They often like to assume the role of commander, constantly giving commands to the dog. As a result the dog will soon lose their enthusiasm for learning. In this the dog is not unlike a child who is constantly being told what they may or may not do.

Greeting rituals

In many families the greeting ritual runs approximately as follows: the door opens, the dog, full of joy, comes running towards you, jumps up at everybody, children are bumped into, and it is nearly impossible to take off jackets and shoes, because the dog is so excited that they keep running between everyone's legs. Getting annoyed with the dog is an almost foregone conclusion. Often it results in action, too. In the hope of preventing the undesired behaviour, the dog is scolded and pushed away. Wouldn't it be nice if the greeting ritual were to happen differently, without all the fuss and annoyance?

Just teach the dog to observe a calm greeting ritual that is carried out in the living area rather than in the entrance.

This is how it's done:

Upon returning home you only give attention to your dog for a brief moment, by saying 'hello' for instance. Afterwards you ignore the dog, take off your coat calmly and proceed to the living room. The dog is greeted properly by everyone only once they are all inside. However, please don't forget the hello at the beginning, because the dog has been waiting for you for such a long time and they would not understand if you were to ignore them completely.

Soon the dog will have learned that after the initial hello they will only get attention once you are in the living room. They will quickly bounce off and expect you there. If your dog becomes boisterous during the ensuing greeting ritual, turn away for a moment and wait until they have calmed down.

You must ask all your visitors to adhere to this greeting procedure as well, otherwise the dog will not stick to the learned behaviour.

Don't jump up at me!

'What a naughty dog!' 'The dog is dominant!' You often hear this being said when a dog jumps up at a human being. This is the result of a classic misunderstanding, because the dog has no other intention than to greet the human being politely.

Among dogs, licking the corners of the mouth of another dog is not a gesture of dominance, but a submissive greeting ritual. We humans are relatively tall, which makes it difficult for a dog to lick the cor-

This is not how it should be! With large heavy dogs in particular it is unpleasant, and it can be dangerous too if they jump up at small children.

ners of our mouths – they have to jump up to reach their target. Often we unwittingly reinforce the dog's behaviour. Children and adults alike tend to find it cute when a puppy jumps up at them. They reward the puppy by stroking them and sometimes they actively encourage them. The little dog is being successful with their behaviour and will display it increasingly often. Once the puppy has become an adult, we humans find the dog jumping up at us unpleasant. We try to push them away with our hands, often accompanied by a 'No!' or 'Get off!'. This is exactly the sort of behaviour that the dog will interpret as an invitation to carry on, rather than as a defensive gesture. The dog cannot understand the words, and all you are demonstrating to them is that their behaviour is rewarded with attention.

 Tip

Try to do it differently. When greeting your dog, immediately go down into a squatting position, and offer them your cheek in a way they can easily reach it. What happens? The dog will instantly begin to lick your face. Will the dog jump up against you? No, why should they? In this position they can greet you in true canine fashion.

Prevent your dog from jumping up at you from day one, no matter whether the dog you have taken in is a puppy or an older dog. Unlike the shaking of hands it is, after all, not a part of the human greeting ritual, and licking the corners of the mouth is unacceptable to most people on the grounds of hygiene. Your guests probably won't be too enthusiastic about a dog jumping up at them, and for small children in particular there is the risk of injury from the dog's nails, and from being knocked over by the sheer weight of the dog.

Prevention, on the other hand, does not mean that your child should use force against the dog. It is not just inappropriate to knee the dog in the chest, to tread on their paws or to pull them down by their collar or harness, but completely ineffective. We humans find this hard to imagine, but the dog would feel affirmed in their behaviour by such actions – they have got the desired attention, albeit in an unpleasant way.

This is how it's done:
Never touch your dog when they jump up at you. Fold your arms and turn your back on the dog without making a comment. This will turn jumping up into a failure for the dog, because they don't get the desired attention. As soon as your dog has all four paws on the ground again, turn towards them and praise them. You have to assume a squatting position for this, because if you praise the dog whilst standing up, they will interpret this as an invitation to jump up at you once more. Practise with your child exactly how they should behave. However, caution is required in the case of toddlers, who are neither tall enough nor stable enough on their feet to prop up the weight of a dog jumping up at them without toppling over. You have to be quick to intervene and protect the child.

Staying safe while out walking

In our present-day society it is necessary in many situations to keep a dog on a leash. This

Both are enjoying themselves here. If the dog isn't too strong and walks on a loose leash, a small child can lead them for a short while. However, you should always stay close at hand.

is not just for the protection of the dog and other animals, but to provide visible relief to a lot of people who feel more comfortable if they can be sure that the approaching dog cannot get too close to them. Older children from the age of fifteen can be allowed to walk on their own with a dog on a leash, provided that the two of them get on with each other and that the dog is not too large or too strong. Younger children aren't able to anticipate danger soon enough, they don't have the experience or the strength, and they also often lack the nerve to deal with a tricky situation. Ask yourself whether your child is strong enough to prevent the dog from running across the road when they spot their best friend on the other side. Also ask yourself whether the child would be able to keep their nerve if another dog were to attack their pet. Especially when they are worried about their own dog's safety, children are often unable to cope.

If you come to the conclusion that your child will not be able to handle this and similar situations, it is too risky to let them take the dog for walks unaccompanied. Instead you could give them the opportunity to enrol for a special young dog-handler class at a dog-training school. There your child will learn how to handle the leash confidently and can practise the correct response to tricky situations.

To prevent your child feeling disappointed because they are not yet allowed to take the dog for walks on their own, you can have them carry out little tasks before and during each walk. For example, the child can put the harness on the dog and attach the leash to it, and your child will probably be pleased if they are allowed occasionally to reward the dog with a treat for walking on the leash like a good dog without pulling.

Getting the dog used to walking on a loose leash is most important in making walks on the leash an enjoyable experience for all involved. If this works really well, even a small child can proudly lead their dog on the leash for a short while now and again. This of course should only be done when the dog is walking in a relaxed manner and you are close at hand.

 Tip

It is best to use a soft leather leash on all your walks. This type of leash has the advantage that it doesn't cut into the flesh if the dog does pull hard for some reason and the leash slips through the child's fingers. Flexible leashes are not suitable. The dog can put a distance of several metres between themselves and the child, and will be almost impossible to control.

This is how it's done:
The dog can learn to walk on a loose leash while still a puppy. The first step is that you don't allow yourself to be pulled. Every time the little dog pulls the leash tight, you or your child stops immediately and waits until the dog has taken a step backwards of their own accord, so the leash hangs loose again. As soon as the leash is loose, you carry on walking straight away. If the puppy stays put, please don't drag them behind you, but wait calmly for them to catch up with you, even if the leash is tightened. Don't lure the puppy to come to you. They will only get your attention if they walk on a loose leash level with you. The dog will soon understand what you want them to do.

This form of training with the leash also works with an older dog. However, if the dog is in the habit of pulling too strongly, you should not do this exercise on your own but seek professional help.

Learning game

This partnership game enables children to experience how a dog may feel who is dragged on a leash.

One child plays the dog, let's call him Max, and ties the leash round his waist; a second child plays the person in charge of the dog, Lisa, who takes the leash in her hand. Treats are laid out on the ground that Max is supposed to pick up and eat while Lisa is dragging him behind her on the leash without paying any attention to him. Next build an obstacle course. Now Max is supposed to negotiate the obstacle course, but is simply dragged across the obstacles by Lisa.

After each child has played Max and Lisa respectively, ask the children how they felt when they were Max. Ask the children to think how and where Max could have hurt himself on the obstacles, and also explain to them that dogs leave their 'news' behind everywhere they go, which needs to be 'read' – and that's why dogs always have their nose close to the ground, sniffing everything. One ought not to disturb them during this activity –would any of the children want to be disturbed while reading an exciting book?

Finally encourage both children to try and think of ways it could be done better.

This is how it's done. Sidney takes the treat carefully out of the child's open palm.

How to give treats properly

Dogs love treats and children love to feed dogs. The child's enjoyment will be short-lived, however, if the dog's behaviour is too rough and excited and they snap at the treat in the child's hand. Your child will soon become scared of the dog.

For this reason, first of all the dog will have to learn that they ought to pick up the treat very gently and without using their teeth. A dog should never take the treat of their own accord, but always wait until they are asked to do so. Only allow your child to feed treats to the dog once they have understood this.

A treat should always be offered in the open palm; never hold it with your fingers. In this way you will avoid painful consequences should the dog forget to be careful at some point.

Important

It should be common practice to allow children to feed dogs only with the express permission of an adult and under adult supervision.

Training in how to give treats is very useful for everyday life with your child and dog. Once the dog has learned to take treats only when asked to do so, they will be less likely to snap other tasty morsels out of your child's hand that aren't meant for them at all.

This is how it's done:
Hold the treat in front of your dog's nose. If the dog tries to take the treat with their teeth, immediately withdraw your hand. Hold your hand out towards them once more, and when the dog approaches the treat, say 'Careful!' If the dog tries again to take it with their teeth, withdraw your hand. They will quickly understand how to get the treat: they get it only if they take it gently!

Once this exercise works reliably, you can proceed to the next step. The dog has to learn only to take the food when asked to do so. For this, hold the treat in your open palm, but hold on to it with your thumb. If the dog tries to take the treat, make a fist immediately and wait until they take a step backwards.

Only when the dog does so should you open your fist again. Repeat this until your dog stops trying to get the treat from you unprompted, but is instead looking at you

expectantly. Now open your hand while at the same time saying 'Take it.' Practise this several times a day in order to firm up this behaviour, and always insist that the dog takes the treat very carefully.

That's my toy!

The dog has stolen a shoe or a toy and carries their conquest around with them. The child runs after the dog screaming in order to retrieve their property. This is a classical situation that almost every dog-owning family will have first-hand experience of. All the angry shouting and running after the dog is a waste of time: they don't in the least intend to give up their prey voluntarily, especially as they are enjoying this chasing game immensely. At last something has interrupted the boredom; everybody's eyes are on them. After this success the dog will continue to steal things in order to have another round of fun.

But for your child this is not a game. They are worried about their possession, and will attempt anything to rescue it. This can turn nasty, because if the child corners the dog in the process, cutting off their escape route, the dog may defend their conquest. The dog is, after all, unaware that this is your child's favourite toy, they only know that their prey is being taken away with the use of force.

To prevent this situation from happening in the first place, it is best to teach your child not to leave their toys lying around. That would remove any temptation for the dog. However, if your dog does manage to snatch something forbidden, your child can offer them a deal. The dog will get something better in return for the snatched item, a treat or their own favourite toy for example.

This method promises a far greater chance of success and is less dangerous than screaming and running after the dog. Your child can practise these swapping deals so they know how to react if the dog really does have a forbidden object in their mouth.

This is how it's done:

If the dog has a toy in their mouth, the child takes the other end in their hand. Now the child shows the dog a second toy or a treat and encourages the dog to let go of the toy they are holding. At the precise moment that the dog opens their mouth, your child gives the signal 'Let go!', and gives the dog friendly praise.

At the beginning it is very important that the dog gets something in return for letting go of the object, to show them that this is not just about something being taken away from them. Soon the dog will let go of things voluntarily, and after a while they don't have to be given a treat every time.

Zeus still has the toy rope in his mouth. Marlies is offering him the giraffe in exchange.

Zeus takes the new toy, having lost any interest in the rope.

It worked! Both parties are happy.

Child and dog at dog-training school

Perhaps you are familiar with this situation: your child simply doesn't follow your advice regarding the dog, or may even believe they know best. In this case it would make good sense to enrol your child and dog in a dog-training school, and of course to accompany them there. Usually children have no problem accepting instruc-tions and tips for dealing with dogs if they come from a trainer in a dog-training school. Be sure to take advantage of this assistance. It will make your job a lot easier, and it is also in the best interest of the dog.

Find a dog-training school where you feel that you and your child will be taken good care of. The classes on offer should have one trainer for a maximum of six human-and-dog pairs. This is the only way the trainer is able to spend enough time and attention on each pair. Do ask questions about the training methods, and also listen to your inner voice. If you, your child or your dog are not happy, try to find an alternative trainer.

Once the right trainer has been found, with professional tuition your child and dog can have a lot of fun together, and develop into a great team.

 Tip

Many dog-training schools offer special dog-handling classes for children. With professional tuition your child will learn how to deal with their dog safely and in the correct manner. Ask specifically for these classes.

David and Shiva are enjoying their joint training sess-ions. The 'sit' exercise is already working well.

Tricks – fun for child and dog

It's got to be fun!

Play and fun, that's what children want to have with their dogs. In the following chapter I'd like to present some ideas for playtime and a few easy to teach tricks tailored to the needs of children and dogs. These should guarantee fun and excitement for all involved.

All games should be supervised by an adult, and it is particularly important with action games such as tug-of-war that each session is kept quite short to prevent the playing partners from getting too boisterous. In the heat of the moment it is possible for both child and dog to overstep the mark, and for the game to get out of control. In this case a quick intervention is necessary in order to prevent the fun turning into a painful experience.

Important

If the dog is over-enthusiastic and snaps at the child's hands, the game has to be interrupted immediately. This way the dog will learn that every time they use their teeth the fun is over, and they will soon get out of the habit of snapping. If the child behaves in a rough manner, this should also mean an end to the playing session.

Tug-of-war

Tug-of-war games with a piece of rope, with the child holding on to one end and the dog on to the other, are popular with children and dogs alike. However, these should only be played under the supervision of an adult who has experience with dogs, because they are not completely without risk.

A dog can quickly get carried away while playing and dash excitedly towards the child in order to fetch the coveted piece of rope, injuring the child with their teeth or toppling them over with their body weight. Dogs can also be injured during tug-of-war games. Older children, in particular, sometimes pull the rope so hard that a small dog or a puppy is flung into the air. There is a considerable risk of injury to the dog.

The one basic prerequisite for a tug-of-war game is that, in order to keep the game under control, your dog must readily

David and Zeus are playing with the rope. Both are still a little hesitant.

respond to the commands 'Take!' and 'Let go!', so play can be interrupted with a 'Let go!' if necessary.

This is how it's done:

For training purposes your child should take a few largish treats in one hand. In the other hand they hold a toy rope or a similar toy, which should have a minimum length of 30 centimetres in order to allow a sufficient safety distance between the child's hand and the dog's teeth.

The child waves the rope in front of the dog's nose until the dog takes it into their mouth. At exactly this moment your child says 'Take!' The dog will instantly embark on a tug-of-war game which the child joins in with for the time being. After a short time the child stops pulling without letting go of the toy rope, and holds a treat in front of the dog's nose. At the precise moment that the dog opens their mouth, your child says 'Let go!', and gives them the treat. This sequence has to be repeated several times in order to demonstrate to the dog that the toy isn't taken away from them for good, but that the game will start afresh as soon as they have let go of the rope.

Fetch!

I would advise against ball throwing games that involve the dog running madly back and forth. Although children and dogs are

Jan has asked the shorthair collie Shiva to adopt the 'sit' position, and shows her the ball.

Now he puts the ball down. Meanwhile Shiva is waiting patiently for Jan to return to her and give the command to go.

Shiva happily returns the ball.

equally enthusiastic about games such as these, the risk of injury to the dog should not be underestimated. The dog's joints are put under too much strain, and spinal injuries are a common occurrence when a dog turns awkwardly while jumping after a ball. In addition many dogs develop into virtual ball junkies, who suffer permanent stress because they are constantly waiting for flying balls, and are unable to play any other games.

If you do play ball games, they should be played as fetch games. For this the ball is laid down or thrown while the dog waits calmly. The dog is only allowed to run and fetch the ball after a command is given. This introduces an element of calmness into the game, while at the same time promoting the dog's control over their own impulses. In her book 'Playtime for Your Dog', Christina Sondermann describes this very poignantly: 'During a walk off the leash a deer suddenly jumps across the path – and instead of chasing after it head over heels, the dog stops and "asks" their human for permission.

This sort of thing is evidence of good impulse control – the ability to exert self-control. Basically, more impulse-control on the part of the dog means that less control from you is needed – and the dog is also going to be more reliable in every-day life situations.'

You will find many further instructions for sensible training and learning games in the above-mentioned book. Children can play many of these games with the dog as well.

This is how it's done:
For this your dog should be able to stay in the 'sit' position, even when you or your child are moving away from them. If the dog is not yet able to do this exercise reliably, you can hold them in place.

After your child has asked the dog to assume the 'sit' position, the child moves a few metres away from the dog, puts the ball down, and returns to the dog. When the child has reached the dog they wait for a few seconds before giving the command to go ahead. Only then is the dog allowed to fetch the ball. As a verbal signal you can use commands such as 'Go', 'Fetch', or simply 'Ball'.

Scrapping, wrestling, catch-me-if-you-can

Children would like to play with dogs as they would with children of the same age. Scrapping and playful wrestling are part of their repertoire. You should not allow them to play such fighting games with dogs, however, especially if the dog involved is a puppy. The young dog would learn from a young age that they are allowed to play roughly with children. What may be fun with a puppy often turns into a serious problem when the dog concerned is an adult and much larger. The game easily becomes too wild, and can become dangerous. Nor should you allow catch-me-if-you-can games, although they are ever popular with children. At first glance they usually seem fun, but with a dog they

Better not! Children should not play wrestling games even with a cute puppy.

can promote the instinct to hunt and catch prey. The excited dog may attempt to snap at the child with their teeth and not to let go, or they may jump up at the child from behind, which can cause a serious fall, especially if smaller children are involved. In addition a dog that has been allowed to play catch-me-if-you-can games with children will not just run after children they know, but will pursue strange children as well. It would be far better if you and your child were to think of some risk-free games that are fun for child and dog.

Scenting games

The nose is a dog's most important sense organ. The inhaled scents help them to find their way around the environment. With their sense of smell a dog can perceive scents far more distincly than we humans can. Scenting games are a brilliant way to occupy a dog; they present a mental challenge to the dog and make them calmer and more balanced. For children too, scenting games are an exciting alternative to wild and uncontrolled chasing games. The child is occupied intensively with their dog, and develops a greater understanding of the dog as a result.

Children particularly enjoy watching their dog search for objects. A dog can learn, for instance, how to search for a particular toy, or to fetch exactly the toy the child wants from several toys lying next to each other.

The advantage of scenting games is that they can be played outside on a sunny day, and just as easily indoors when it's raining.

Hiding games are enjoyed by children and dogs alike! Marlies is about to hide the toy in the undergrowth. Then Zeus is supposed to search for it.

This is how it's done:

There are several different ways to encourage your dog to search for an object. I would like to introduce a version that is easier for children.

Together with your child, think about names to give to the toys that you want to practise with. Your child takes one of the toys and encourages the dog to take it. As soon as the dog takes it into their mouth your child immediately says the name of the respective toy, praises the dog enthusiastically, and uses the toy to play with the dog.

After a few repetitions the dog will understand, and your child can begin to put the toy on the ground somewhere close to them, while you gently hold on to the dog. Then you let the dog go, while at the same time the child says the name of the toy, for example 'Croco' for a soft toy crocodile. Does the dog run up to the crocodile and take it in their mouth straight away? Excellent! This is the first step. In order to see whether the dog has understood the difference between their 'Croco' and the other toys, your child puts the crocodile on the ground with one or two other toys. The toys should be placed at some distance from each other. Now the child gives the dog the signal 'Croco' once again. It is important not to assist the dog in their search, but to let them work on their own. If the dog also fetches the correct toy this time around, your child has done it! Now the same exercise can be repeated using different toys.

If your child places all their toys in front of the dog, and the dog still manages to pick the desired toy, now that would be showing off! For the dog the game becomes even more interesting if your child hides the toys and asks the dog to search for them.

Tip

Many dog-training schools now offer special classes for scenting work. Once your child is a bit older and enjoys searching games with the dog, why not suggest to them that they enrol in a scenting class together with the dog?

Interactive toys

It's not only the scenting games described above that represent calm, but exciting, alternatives to the more sporting fetching and tug-of-war games.

The interactive toys that have recently become available in pet shops, often made of wood or plastic, also offer interesting

This requires a little brain power. Shiv can smell the treat and is thinking hard about how to extract it.

ways of keeping a dog busy. These also require more brain than brawn. There are a few variations, but the basic principle is always similar. Pre-prepared openings are filled with treats and the dog has to perform tasks of varying degrees of difficulty in order to reach the treats. The dog may have to knock over blocks that have been placed over the openings, roll away balls, or pull a drawer with a rope attached to it out of a box.

You will find addresses for online retailers who sell various interactive toys in the Appendix.

Going for walks

Walks should always be totally dedicated to the dog. If we don't interact with the dog we are boring walking partners for them. They will soon turn to more interesting things such as hunting, or running towards other people and dogs.

 Important
Before you allow the dog to walk without a leash you should be confident that they will return to you at any time without fail when you call them.

Joint games make walks into a true experience for the child and the dog alike. Here are a few ideas that make for exciting excursions:

- **Searching for people:** Hold on to the dog while your child hides behind a tree and calls the dog. Now send the dog off to search for the child.
- **Overcoming obstacles:** Child and dog climb over tree trunks, large rocks or piles of grit together.
- **Fetch:** Your child prompts the dog to 'sit' or 'down' again and again during a walk, and places a toy on the ground that the dog fetches on command. Note that dogs generally don't like to sit or lie down on stony or hard surfaces.
- **Searching for treats or toys:** The dog waits until the child has hidden a treat or a toy. They are then allowed to search for it.

Tricks – great fun for all

Children and dogs simply love tricks! Practising tricks isn't just great fun for all involved, but requires a lot of brain power on the part of the dog. Learning tricks provides the dog with an intellectual challenge. The joint training efforts also serve to deepen the bond between child and dog.

In order to enable the child and dog to enjoy a few early successes, I have chosen three from a huge range of possible tricks that are particularly easy to learn. The important thing is that your child practises the tricks with the dog in small steps and that the child doesn't demand the dog's

Learning Game

The tree of treats

This used to be my son Lukas' favourite game. Take several largish pieces of cooked sausage with you on a walk. Somewhere on your way tie the dog to a tree or distract them in order to allow your child to walk ahead and attach the sausage pieces to the end of some branches on a bush. Some should be at a height that is within easy reach for the dog, others a little higher. The child must make sure that the ends of the branches aren't too pointy, otherwise the dog may be hurt. When they have finished doing this your child should come back to you and then discover the sausage bush together with the dog. Now your dog can enjoy eating the treats off the bush. In order to reach the higher sausage pieces the dog needs the help of your child who has to bend the branches down for them. This way the dog learns that they need a human in order to reach all the treats. You will soon notice that the dog will seek your child's company more and more often in the hope of discovering another tree of treats.

Marlies attaches the sausage pieces at varying heights on the branches of a bush.

Zeus has eaten all the treats that were at the right height for him to reach. Now Marlies is bending the branches down, helping him to reach the sausage pieces that were attached a little higher up in the bush.

attention for more than five to ten minutes at a time. Impatience doesn't get you anywhere. Only one trick should be practised in each session. Begin practising a new trick only when the dog is able to perform one trick confidently; anything else would confuse the dog and be disappointing for both parties.

Tip
Dogs and children are only able to concentrate for a limited period of time. Short learning sessions (five to ten minutes per day) are therefore much more sensible and effective than long ones.

Dogs of all ages absolutely love to do trick training. There is no age limit, but bear in mind that puppies don't have the ability to concentrate for as long as adult dogs, and aren't able to learn difficult tricks.

Tricks that involve high or long jumps should also not be practised by puppies or juvenile dogs. The joints, which are still soft at this young age, may suffer permanent damage. The potential health problems of older dogs also have to be taken into account.

If you notice that your dog is suffering any pain or discomfort while carrying out a particular trick, please break off this exercise. There are so many different tricks, you can be sure to find a number of other tricks that are more suitable for your dog.

Important
Don't train on a full stomach. Just as with all other exercise sessions, before you begin practising any tricks your dog should not have eaten anything for two to three hours beforehand, otherwise there is a risk of causing stomach ache and vomiting. In the *worst case scenario, particularly important with large breeds, there is a risk of the stomach of the dog accidentally becoming twisted, a potentially life-threatening condition.*

The handshake

The handshake is a simple trick that even puppies are able to learn easily. Your child will be really proud if their dog greets relatives and friends by offering their paw to them.

This is how it's done:

The child asks the dog to assume the 'sit' position in front of them. Now the child takes a treat in their hand, making a fist around it while the dog is watching them, then the child extends their closed fist to the dog. The dog will first sniff the hand and then try to get to the treat. At this exact moment, while the dog uses his paw and scratches at the child's fist, the action is affirmed with 'Yes', or 'Nice'. The dog will not get the treat from that fist, though, but from the other hand. This has the advantage that the dog doesn't assume that he has to 'dig' the treat out of the hand. The dog will then find it easier when the child offers only an empty hand later on.

This exercise is repeated many times until the dog puts their paw on the fist without hesitation. Now the child can just hold out an empty open hand without a treat.

As soon as the dog reliably does the handshake every time you hold your hand towards them, the child can simultaneously say 'hello' each time. Soon the dog

Jan has hidden a treat in his fist. This encourages Shiva to put her paw on his fist.

After a few practice sessions, Shiva has mastered the perfect greeting.

will recognise this word as the signal for the handshake.

 Tip
Often dogs do the handshake without having learned it beforehand. In this case you only have to link the voluntary handshake

with a command, and the dog will soon do it as soon as the child asks them to.

The roll-over

This trick involves the dog doing a complete roll-over. The starting position for the

Jan practises the roll-over with Zeus. He skilfully guides the treat in such a way that Zeus first drops on to his side and then rolls over his back.

roll-over is 'down'. Your dog should be able to carry out this exercise reliably before you start.

This is how it's done:
Your child asks the dog to assume the 'down' position and kneels in front of them. Then the child takes a treat and guides it in a semi-circular movement from the dog's nose towards the shoulder blade. The dog has to turn on to its side in order to keep an eye on the treat. Even just this first step is rewarded with a treat. Next your child continues moving the treat across the dog's body, slowly enough that the dog is able to follow it with their eyes.

As soon as they have turned on to their other side, the dog gets a reward. The treat for the intermediate step is gradually given less often now, and in the end the dog gets a reward only when they have rolled over completely. Once the dog is able to do the exercise without the treat for the intermediate step and does a complete roll-over without hesitation, your child just gives the signal 'roll'. This trick is even more impressive if the dog does the roll-over when prompted by just a hand movement.

 Tip
As an alternative, a child can also teach 'playing dead'. For this, the dog only rolls on to its side, and doesn't do a complete roll-over. After the first step for the roll-over this goal is almost reached – the dog is lying on its side. After a few successful practice sessions your child can introduce the verbal signal 'Bang!'.

Jumping through a hoop
For this trick you need a hula-hoop. Once the dog has learned to jump reliably through the hoop, child and dog can wow their audience with a performance worthy of a circus act. It is even more spectacular if the dog jumps through a hoop that is covered with sheets of paper.

This is how it's done:
Your child puts the hoop on the ground, holding it upright, and with the help of a treat lures the dog through. When they have reached the other side of the hoop, the dog gets the treat. In this way first of all the dog gets familiar with the hoop. After repeating this two to three times your child can hold the hoop about five centimetres above the ground, and ask the dog to jump through it. Every time the dog jumps, the child gives the command 'hop'. This step should also be repeated two to three times. Once the dog is happy to jump through the hoop, your child can hold the hoop a little higher, depending on the dog's age and size.

For a rather spectacular version of this trick you need a few sheets of colourful tissue paper. From this your child cuts several strips, ten centimetres wide, three of which are attached to the hoop. Next the child asks the dog to jump through the hoop several times. Once this is working well, more and more strips are added, until the dog jumps through a hoop completely full of paper strips without hesitation. Only afterwards is the entire hoop covered with tissue paper. A long cut in the centre of the paper makes the exercise easier for the dog. Your child sticks

At the beginning Jaqueline uses a treat to lure the border collie Angelo through the hoop on the ground.

After repeating this a few times Angelo jumps through the hoop without any treat.

their hand through this cut, holding the treat, luring the dog through the hoop. Make sure that the dog is not showing any signs of fear as they tear the paper. If they do, you can make several cuts in the paper in order to make the exercise easier for the dog. Be-fore the last step is attempted, the jump through the papered hoop, walking slowly through the hoop should be practised many times.

Even if your dog is able to manage the jump confidently, you should still make at least one cut in the paper. This makes it a lot easier for the dog to carry out the trick.

 Real life dog stories

When our son Lukas was practising tricks with our dog Foxi, it was great to see the amount of patience Lucas was able to muster for this task, and how much fun the two were having together. They were both pleased with the tiniest of successes, and Foxi got a lot of treats. Lukas was mightily proud of his dog when he was able to perform the tricks they had practised, and the other children were simply agog.

The girl is a little scared of the border collie, but with the support of her mother, who has put her arm around her protectively, she dares to walk a little closer to the dog.

When children are scared of dogs

Many children are pleased when they meet a dog. They feel a special attraction to these animals. But what can be done if things are different for your child?

What is fear and where does it come from?

Fear is certainly not a pleasant feeling, but it is a natural one that plays an important part in the lives of our children. Normal fear, or to put it differently, healthy caution, prevents children entering into situations that represent a threat to their well being and that they can't cope with. Intrepid children are less good at risk assessment, and as a result get into difficulties more often.

However, children can also learn fear from their parents or other people close to them. A person who has had a bad experience with dogs, and as a result suffers a sense of fear or at least insecurity when confronted with a dog, will not be able to hide this from their child. Children have very sensitive radar, and are able to sense such fears.

Many parents also express their fear in a very tangible manner. With the words 'Be careful', 'Move away' or 'We don't know whether he will bite', they keep their children away from dogs and reinforce their fear of these animals.

Another reason for such anxieties may be negative personal experience. The trigger doesn't always have to be something as bad as a dog bite. A child having been bumped into or knocked over by a boisterous dog in an unpleasant manner while playing is often sufficient.

 Important

Respect your child's fear and don't make fun of them. Don't force your child into contact with dogs, but convey to them that there is nothing wrong with being scared of dogs, and help them overcome their fear in a sensitive manner.

My child is scared – what can I do?

When children who suffer from a fear of dogs come across a dog they often react with panic, scream and run away. In most dogs this triggers a playing instinct, or a hunting instinct – they run after the child, which increases the child's fear even more. In a situation like this, it is not very helpful if you react in a hectic manner yourself, and scold the child, the dog or the dog owner. Instead it would be better to try and calm your child down, and don't hesitate to let approaching dog owners know that your child is scared of dogs, and ask them if they don't mind putting their dog on a leash. Most dog owners will be glad to oblige and call their dog.

If you want to help your child overcome their fear, the most important thing is to explain things to them, because fear is often just the fear of the unknown, things you can't fathom. If your child finds out as much as possible about this unknown, and therefore scary, creature, the dog, and learns to understand canine behaviour and put it into perspective, they will soon feel more at ease.

If your child's fear is so pronounced that they begin to avoid everyday situations because of their fear of dogs, you should ask for help from a professional therapist. After all, it is almost impossible to avoid coming into contact with dogs more completely, they are everywhere. You are also running the risk that your child may divert away from their safe route home from school to avoid a dog who may come towards them there every day, or that they may jump into the road in a panic when chancing upon a dog on the pavement. Children learn very quickly to overcome their fear as a result of interacting with well trained dogs under professional supervision. Take advantage of this opportunity!

 Tip

If you are the owner of a child-friendly dog, you should not forget that there are children, as well as adults, who are scared of dogs. Please bear this in mind and put your dog on a leash when somebody is passing you in the opposite direction.

Even though this dog looks friendly enough with his toy in his mouth, it is possible that he may not like children.

Are strange dogs suitable play-mates for children?

Children often feel an almost magical attraction towards strange dogs, and are bent on stroking them and playing with them.

Especially irresistible are puppies and dogs who are carrying toys in their mouths. However, it is best not to allow your child to play with strange dogs. Because the child and the dog are not familiar with each other there is a risk that the child may make an unexpected movement that will cause the dog to feel insecure, or startle the dog, and prompt them to take defensive action. A harmless game can turn into a nightmare.

This applies even if a dog appears to be friendly and nice. We cannot judge just from looking at a dog whether their past experience with children has been positive, and that the dog will react in a friendly manner. On the contrary, the dog may have some unpleasant memory associated with a child, making them scared of children in general. The behaviour of strange dogs is almost impossible to predict.

 Important

Children should always treat strange dogs with caution and respect, and not see them as potential playmates.

Dogs on a leash

A first cautious contact: the dog is allowed to sniff the child's hand.

When children come across a dog on a leash they often run towards them without asking first, wanting to stroke the dog. Usually this happens so fast that the dog's owner has no time to react. This isn't just potentially risky, it's simply impolite. Many dog owners don't want their dog to be stroked by strangers at all, and this should be respected. A dog is a living being and not a cuddly soft toy that can be touched at any time by anybody, no matter how nice and child-friendly the dog may be.

Out of politeness, as well as for their own protection, your child has to learn that they must always ask permission before stroking a dog, as a matter of principle.

A strange dog on a leash who is waiting for their owner in front of a supermarket

This is the right thing to do. The boy stays calm, turns his head away and lets his arms hang by his side. The dog will soon lose interest.

must never be touched or, especially, taunted. Because of the leash the dog has no room for evasive movements to avoid the contact foisted upon them.

This is how it's done:

If the owner has agreed to have their dog stroked your child should not walk up to the dog straight away, but must give the dog the chance to sniff their hand first. This gives the dog the opportunity to decide whether they want to approach or not. To do this the child assumes a squatting position in front of the

dog and stretches their hand out towards the dog close to the ground, without touching the dog. Normally the dog will then establish contact of their own accord by sniffing the hand. Now the child can approach the dog cautiously from the side, squat down again and stroke the dog on their side or chest.

 Important
Children should only be allowed to touch a strange dog if the owner has given express permission.

Encounters with free-running dogs

Normally a free-running dog is not interested in an unknown human, at least not while the human is behaving in an inconspicuous manner. But this is exactly what children don't do. As soon as they spot a dog from afar they either make an enthusiastic dash towards it, or they run away from it because they're scared, equally drawing the dog's attention towards them. The dog will react according to its nature. A child who is running away may arouse the dog's playing or hunting instincts, which will make them run after the child.

A child rushing towards the dog may make them feel threatened and they may try to defend themselves. The dog has no way of knowing whether the child has good intentions towards them. In the past the dog may have been mistreated by a child wearing similar clothes, and they may therefore assume that all children who look like this have to be treated with extreme caution.

This is how it's done:
When encountering a free-running dog your child should above all stay calm, no matter whether the dog appears friendly or threatening. The child should avert their gaze from the dog, ignore the dog, and let their arms hang down by the sides of their body. If your child is holding an object in their hand, they must drop it immediately in order to avoid giving the dog a reason to jump up at them. Normally the dog will soon lose interest and turn away. If this is not the case your child should slowly turn away, with as few movements as possible, and move away from the dog.

If your child happens to be on a bicycle during an encounter with a free-running dog, they should ride past the dog very slowly. It is best if the child stops pedalling, and lets the bike roll past the dog. However, if the dog chases after your child, the child should brake abruptly, get off the bike and stand behind the bicycle. In this case it is also important that the child stays completely calm and doesn't look at the dog.

If your child falls over because they have tripped, or they can't control the bike, or they are pushed over by the dog, they must roll into a ball and protect their neck and face with their arms.

 Tip

Make sure you practise the correct behaviour towards free-running dogs by simulating the real thing. Your child will feel more confident and safe during an unexpected encounter with a strange dog as a result.

Leave dogs in backyards and gardens alone!

Dogs are often found on their own without their owners in fenced-off gardens and backyards. If your child gets too close to the fence during a walk, for example, the dog may come rushing towards them, barking. A dog considers the house, the backyard and the garden as their territory; and it is their nature to defend this territory against intruders. Your child should respect this and calmly walk past the property without paying any attention to the dog. The child must certainly not annoy the dog unnecessarily by throwing objects at them, or otherwise teasing or taunting them. Dogs have a very good memory, and you never know, one day you may meet this particular dog in the street.

They will remember this unpleasant situation and behave aggressively towards the child.

 Important

Your child must never trespass on to a strange property that has a dog in residence, even when they have thrown their favourite ball over the fence during play. In this situation the child should always ask the owner of the dog to return the ball.

It is very dangerous for children to try to separate fighting dogs.

Fighting dogs

Dogs like to play with other dogs, and on occasion a harmless game can turn serious. Before you know it there is a boisterous scrap going on.

If a child sees this, it is possible that they may approach the combatants wanting to mediate in the quarrel. In particular, if their own dog is involved in the scrap, your child will be very scared for their pet, and will want to rescue them. Don't let a child attempt this under any circumstances! Fighting dogs don't hear or see what's going on around them. A dog who is fighting concentrates exclusively on their adversary, and cannot be distracted. During the scrap a dog is blind, deaf and devoid of emotions. It makes no difference whether the dog involved is a strange dog or your own dog. Even your own dog would not be aware if they are biting a hand that is trying to help them. It is extremely difficult even for adults to separate fighting dogs. For children it is utterly impossible and very dangerous!

Often such scraps appear worse than they are. Serious injuries are relatively rare. Usually dogs just want to establish who is the stronger, and they then stop of their own accord.

 Important
When dogs are fighting, children must never interfere.

Children are old enough to grieve when they are old enough to love.

Children saying farewell

My first dog, Sammy, suddenly died aged four. I was twelve years old at the time. He died in the night, and my parents only told me when I returned home from school and when Sammy had already been taken away. I didn't understand the world any more. Why had he left me, how could he do this? We were such good friends! What was I supposed to do without him? What had happened to him? Where was he now? Why couldn't I see him at least one last time and stroke him? Why wasn't I allowed to say goodbye?*

When a dog dies, parents are often at a loss and feel insecure about how to explain to a child the death of their best friend. Many suppress their own feelings because they believe they have to protect their child from the reality of death, in order not to burden them with something they don't yet understand. However, children are confronted with death from an early age and have their own thoughts on the matter. Share your thoughts with your child, before they start to get scared of dying because of their own thoughts and unanswered questions. A dead bird by the side of the road, for instance, may be a good opportunity to raise the subject with your child.

Don't hide your own grief about your dog's death from your child, but grieve together instead. In this way you avoid death being perceived as something horrible that you're not allowed to talk about: 'I understand, I miss Bella too'. 'Do you want to talk about it?' is better than 'Don't be sad'. Don't foist any questions on your child, but always give honest answers to the questions they ask, no matter how old they are. Your child will know when you're lying to them, and they may begin to have doubts about whether you're ever telling the truth.

Avoid circumscribing death. This could cause children to be scared. The explanation: 'Your friend was ill, he has gone to sleep and he is now in animal heaven,' may prompt your child to worry about the possibility that they may die when they are ill, or when they go to sleep. Sentences such as: 'God loved Bella so much, he took her into heaven to be with him,' are only seemingly tailored to the needs of children. As a result your child may wonder whether God will soon take someone else from the family, or even themselves, into heaven.

Death is a part of our lives, and it is important that you convey a natural understanding of death and grief to children. Give your child the opportunity to say goodbye to their dog, and allow them to decide whether they want to be present when the dog is put to sleep, or whether they want to see the dog afterwards for one last time to stroke them.

How to help your child

Children grieve in different ways, some for a short period, some for longer. Some children will even have you believing that they don't grieve at all. But this is not the case. They just blot out their grief, and it is possible that it will surface many years later.

Grieving children often just lose their appetite or stop enjoying their play for a time. Some get angry and loud, or look for someone to blame for what happened. This can be the parents, because in the child's opinion they didn't take enough care of the dog, or the vet, because they were unable to help the dog. Show your child that you know what they mean, and give them the opportunity to express their feelings freely. Relish in sharing your memories. Tell each other about the adventures you had with the dog, and be glad of the many beautiful years you were able to spend together. Write a letter to the dog with your child, or a story about the dog, or draw a picture together – this allows even the smallest children to express their feelings.

It is also helpful if people who are close to the child, such as relatives, teachers and friends, know what has happened. Ask people to understand and support the grieving child. Don't try to replace the deceased dog by a new one in the hope that it will alleviate your child's pain, but wait until your child expresses a desire to have a new dog of their own accord. Children often need quite a long time before they are ready to welcome a new dog into their heart.

The rainbow bridge

When Foxi died and my son Lukas was still small, I read the story about the rainbow bridge to him. I would like you to have this story as a conclusion to this book.

The rainbow bridge

There is a bridge connecting Heaven to Earth. Because of its many colours it is known as the rainbow bridge.

On either side of the bridge lies a land with meadows, hills and juicy green grass. When a beloved animal has gone to sleep forever on Earth, they go to this beautiful place. In this land there is an abundance of food and drink, and the weather is always beautiful, spring-like and warm.

The old and sick animals are young and healthy again. They play together all day long. They are too busy to be lonely.

They miss you, but with the special wisdom that animals have, they have faith that this situation will soon change. And while they're having fun, they are waiting, full of trust.

This way they run and play together every day, until one day one of the animals suddenly stops in their tracks and looks up. Their nostrils flare, they prick up their ears, and their eyes become wide open! Suddenly the animal runs from the middle of the group and flies across the green grass. Their feet carry them faster and faster. They have seen you!

And when you and your beloved animal meet, you take them in your arms and hold them tight. Your face is being kissed, again and again, and you happily gaze into the eyes of your pet at last. They had been gone from your life for so long, but never from your heart. Now you both know that everything is all right.

Together you walk across the rainbow bridge, and you will never be separated again…

Anon

Concluding thoughts

It's done! Until now I was only able to support parents and children in their dealings with dogs within the framework of the courses offered at my dog-training school. This book now makes it possible for me to share my experience with far more people.

It would be nice to think that my book has helped you in your efforts to teach your child a greater understanding of dogs, giving them greater confidence when dealing with dogs,

and that it played a part in making your child and your dog into a great team.

I would really love to receive any feedback regarding my book, and I would also be very happy to answer your questions. You can reach me online: info@spirits-of-life.at.

Now all that's left to do is to wish you a lot of fun and success with this book, and that all your children will enjoy many happy hours with their marvellous canine friends.

Thank you

My first book! It was a beautiful experience for me, and I got a lot of joy out of it. For my husband Georg and my son Lukas and for my two golden retrievers Apollo and Zeus it was not an easy time. My thoughts were exclusively centred on writing; I often even used to wake up at night because I had an idea that I had to write down immediately. I give my special thanks to them. Without their understanding and support I would not have been able to write this book.

I thank all the dogs who have shared my life, and also those whom I was only able to know for a short while. I have learned so much about the wonderful creature that is the dog from all of you.

Dagmar Cutka with her two golden retrievers, Apollo and Zeus.

I'd also like to thank:

The photographer Christiane Slawik: Dear Christiane, you have managed to make this book come to life with your fantastic photos. We thoroughly enjoyed the time that you and your husband Thomas spent with us.

To my proofreader Maren Müller: Dear Maren, you have always supported me with practical advice, and you encouraged me when I had doubts.

Many, many thanks to all the children involved:

Daniel, David, Fabian, Jan, Jan, Jaqueline, Mariella, Marlies, Maximilian, Mia-Anna, Moritz and Raoul.

And the dogs:

Angelo, Balou, Blaze, Cowboy, Daika, Gustav, Mori, Shiva, Sidney, Siri, Sweety, Tigger, Velvet and Yuki, who gave their all despite the exhausting photo shoots.

About the author

Dagmar Cutka lives with her husband and her two dogs in Lower Austria. As a qualified European Dog Trainer she runs the Spirits of Life Hundeschule (dog-training-school) together with her husband. Her main fields of expertise are the interactions between children and dogs and behavioural therapy for dogs. In her training school Dagmar offers classes for child and dog, she also advises families at home, and visits schools and nursery schools with her dogs. She runs special training courses to help children overcome their fear of dogs. Her particular concern is to teach children how to deal with dogs in the appropriate manner and to gain a better understanding of dogs.

Appendix

Useful addresses

Dagmar Cutka
Spirits of Life – Hundeschule
2440 Gramatneusiedl
AUSTRIA
www.spirits-of-life.at
Tel. +43 650 7279969

Pet Dog Trainers of Europe
The European Association of Dog Trainers
for the promotion of a fair and humane
upbringing for dogs.
www.pet-dog-trainers-europe.com

www.companyofanimals.co.uk
Phone 01932 566696

www.dog-games.co.uk
Phone 01684 569553

www.traininglines.co.uk
Phone 0845 6442397

www.positiveanimalsolutions.co.uk
Phone 01652 661951

www.sheilaharper.co.uk
Phone 01543 878989

Further reading

Donaldson, Jean:
The Culture Clash
James and Kenneth Publishers

Lehari, Dr. Gabriele:
Bringing up Puppy
Cadmos Books

McConnell, Patricia:
At the Other End of the Leash
Random House

Pryor, Karen:
**Don't Shoot the Dog –
The new art of teaching and training**
Ringpress Books

Sondermann, Christina:
Playtime for your Dog
Cadmos Books

Zaitz, Manuela:
Trick School for Dogs
Cadmos Books

Index

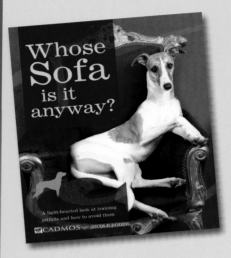

Nicole Röder

WHOSE SOFA IS IT ANYWAY?
A light-hearted look at training pitfalls and how to avoid them

A wry look at training errors from both the human and canine point of view. See through your dog's eyes to learn why tyranny is fun and explore antiquated training methods and the people who support them! This books explains the most common communication mistakes with a healthy dose of humour, suggesting solutions that are easy to implement. With sumptuous illustrations, this book will appeal to every dog owner – and a perfect gift to share with your dog-owning friend!

112 pages, fully illustrated in colour
Softcover with French folds
ISBN 978-3-86127-962-4

Dr. Gabriele Lehari
BRINGING UP PUPPY

It is during the first months of his life that the character and nature of our dogs is largely moulded. This accessible guide provides a wealth of information, helping all new and existing puppy owners enjoy this precious time, and ensuring that their puppy develops into a reliable companion.

96 pages, fully illustrated in colour
Softcover
ISBN 978-3-86127-959-4

Dorothee Dahl
GOOD TIMES WITH OLDER DOGS

This book sets out ideas on how you can make your dog's senior years particularly enjoyable, giving consideration on the older dog's special needs during this life phase. Readers will learn about the right care for older dogs, all the changes that can occur and how to ensure that the senior dog stays fit and healthy for as long as possible.

80 pages, fully illustrated in colour
Softcover
ISBN 978-3-86127-972-3

Christina Sondermann
PLAYTIME FOR YOUR DOG

Games play an important role in the development and well-being of dogs. This book will help discover and employ games and activities on an everyday basis, using everyday objects. These games will not only be enjoyed by both the dog owner and their companion, they will also contribute towards a dog's fitness and training.

128 pages, fully illustrated in colour
Hardcover with jacket
ISBN 978-3-86127-922-8

Monika Gutmann
LINE TRAINING FOR DOGS

Unless they're on a lead, many dogs refuse to come back to their owners, and simply do as they please. Dogs like these commonly spend their lives on leads that are much too short, so are unable to enjoy the privilege of running free. The advice that's often given is to give line training a try. This is the first book published on this subject, which will provide step-by-step guidance on how to perform successful line training with your dog.

96 pages, fully illustrated in colour
Softcover
ISBN 978-3-86127-961-7

CADMOS

www.cadmos.co.uk